ATLANTIC
PUBLISHERS & DISTRIBUTORS (P) LTD
7/22, Ansari Road, Darya Ganj, New Delhi
Tel.: +91-11-4077 5252, 2327 3880
E-mail: orders@atlanticbooks.com
Web: www.atlanticbooks.com

Published by Atlantic Publishers & Distributors (P) Ltd.

Reprinted in 2018, 2019, 2020, 2021, 2022, 2023, 2024, 2025, 2026



Third Edition: 2013
Second Edition: 2005
First Edition: 1998



Printed & bound in India by Atlantic Print Services

To

My Favourite Teacher

Professor M.Q. Khan

and

Members of the Researchers' Association, Odisha, which I founded along with him in 1995

# Preface

My book, *A Handbook of Translation Studies* has gained acceptance all over the country and undergone reprint in 2009 and 2011 since its first publication in 2005. The book has proved to be useful to the students, researchers and teachers of our country. The growing demand for translation studies as a separate discipline in recent years has enhanced the usefulness of this book. Keeping this in mind I enlarged the scope of this book by adding six new chapters to it in second edition. The new chapters were Chapters 9 to 14 which deal with varied topics, "The Role of the Translator", "A Critique of Translation Theories", "Translation Theory and Practice: The Indian Context", "Comparative Literature and Translation Studies: A Correlation", "Translation in the Twenty-First Century: The Global Context", and "From Translation of Bhasa Literature to Comparative Literature and Nation Building". (I have again revised this book and added a new chapter entitled, "Translator's Dilemma: Agony or Ecstasy?" in the third cdition). "Translate and Perish" which I wrote for *The Indian Journal of English* Vol. 46, 2009 as its Chief Editor to underline the importance of translation in our time is included. The Bibliography has been updated for the benefit of readers who seek an introduction to it.

The Researchers' Association, Odisha provided me a forum to deliver plenary lectures on translation studies for the benefit of the researchers from all over the country. I would like to thank all the members of the Researchers'

Association, Odisha, whose interest in the subject became a source of inspiration for me. No wonder, the book is dedicated to them and their President, my revered teacher Professor M.Q. Khan.

Last but not least, I would like to thank Dr. K.R. Gupta, Hon. Advisor, Atlantic Publishers and Distributors (P) Ltd., New Delhi and his staff for bringing out the book in time.

**Bijay Kumar Das**

# Acknowledgements

I take this opportunity to thank all those who helped me in completing the task of writing this book and bringing out its revised and enlarged edition.

Acknowledgements are due to *The Critical Endeavour* and *The Indian Journal of English Studies* in which two articles first appeared.

I am also thankful to Atlantic Publishers and Distributors (P) Ltd., New Delhi for publishing and promoting this book.

**Bijay Kumar Das**

# Translate or Perish

The concept of Indian literature is open to debate, notwithstanding the laudable attempt by Sahitya Akademi to publish all the regional literatures of India under that title in its journal, *Indian Literature.* Indian literature is a multilingual literature. And it is in this sense that Odia literature, Bengali literature, Telugu literature, Tamil literature, Kannada literature, Urdu literature and so on are written in their respective languages. (It is another matter that Hindi literature is written in the Devnagari script.) The question is how the readers of a particular language can read the literature written in another language unless it is translated into that language which they know. For instance, how a Bengali can read Odia literature or a Tamilian read Kannada literature without that literature being translated into his/her language. Even when that is done, the problem is not fully solved. That is because if one literature is translated into another regional language, then only the people belonging to that language will read it, not other people who know some other languages of India. But if a regional literature is translated into English, all the people who know English all over the country, irrespective of region, will read it. There is another angle of this equation, that is, literature presupposes a language and it is also equally true that language is hinged upon a culture. It is in this sense, that Odia literature, Bengali literature, Gujarati literature, Marathi literature, Tamil literature, Telugu literature, Kannada literature and Urdu literature are grounded in their respective cultures. But these cultures are not isolated cultures, they belong to a larger culture—that is Indian culture. The great rivers of our country—Ganga, Jamuna, Narmada, Sindhu, Kaveri, Brahmaputra and Mahanadi—are our common links. Water is the generic force. It is sacred to us. In our great epic *The Mahabharata*, Sanjay describes the nation to Dhritarashtra what *Bharatabarsha* means—the whole country from Kashmir to Kanyakumari. The culture being one, we are divided by languages, which became the medium of literatures.

Now how to make a pan Indian literature, the one like Sanskrit literature which once upon a time was a vibrant literature—now almost reduced to the language of rituals. Which literature can take the place of Sanskrit now? Not any of the regional literatures nor even Indian English literature alone. Therefore, we need all the regional literatures in English translation along with Indian English literature to make pan Indian literature, which can be offered as a course in the Indian universities to make our younger generation aware of Indian traditions, culture and identity. That will be an antidote to the ugly regionalism which is raising its head like a wounded tigress to devour us. Now it is time to translate our literature, our thought or perish.

# Contents

# 1

# Introduction

To give an exact definition or meaning of 'translation' is not an easy task. 'Translation' like poetry has become elusive. It is both a substitution and a transference of meaning from one language (*i.e.,* source language, SL) to another (*i.e.,* target language, TL) and neither. The concept of translation has undergone a sea change over the years. The theories of translation developed from purely linguistic approach of the sixties to textual focus of the seventies, have now yielded place to the culture based theory. The well-known dictum of Benedetto Croce, the Italian Critic: "Traddutore-traditore" (the translator is a traitor, a falsifier of the original) seems to be dated. Equally dated is the cynical observation that "Translation is like a Woman if beautiful, it cannot be faithful and if faithful, it cannot be beautiful"—Anon (Quoted in Krishnaswamy '*et al.*').[1] In the light of recent literary criticism which denies the author, undermines the text, highlights the reader and emphasizes the polysemy of interpretation and pleads for the indeterminacy of meaning, the art of translation has become increasingly difficult.

Translation according to Dr. Johnson involves the process of "change into another language, retaining the sense" which is indeed the basic objective. Modifying this statement A.H. Smith maintains that "to translate is to change into another language retaining as much of the sense as one can."[2] Catford defines translation from the linguistic point of view:

> Translation may be defined as follows: the replacement of textual material in one language (SL) by equivalent material in another language.[3]

Catford adds emphatically:

> The central problem of translation-practice is that of finding TL translation equivalents. A central task of translation theory is that of defining the nature and condition of translation equivalence.[4]

Peter Newmark in his well known piece "The Theory and Practice of Translation" opines that each act of translation involves some loss of the original meaning and this "basic loss of meaning is on a continuum between over translation and under-translation."[5]

Translation has been described variously by several scholars in different places at different points of time. For instance, Theodore Savory defines translation as an 'art,'[6] and Eric Jacobsen defines it as a 'craft,'[7] while Eugene Nida describes it as a 'science'[8] borrowing this concept from the German. Horst Frenz goes a step ahead to accept translation as an 'art' but with qualifications, stating that, "translation is neither a creative art nor an imitative art, but stands somewhere between the two."[9] Though translation has been described differently as an art, a craft and a science, none of these is adequate. On the other hand, each concept expresses the personal prejudice of the person who says so. Art is creative and the expression of beauty. On the other hand, craft has a "lower status occupation" of amateurishness and trickery. The critics' opinion of translation as a purely mechanistic process springs from obsession with science. The distinction between the "creative" and "mechanical" processes is not right. In fact translation is more than all these art, craft and science. It is a process of analysis, interpretation and creation which leads to a replacement of one set of linguistic resources and values for another. In the process part of the original meaning is lost but an easily identifiable core is kept. It is an act of adjustment and a compromising exercise.

J.C. Catford suggested that in translation the meanings of the source language is substituted by the meanings of the target language. Thus, Catford states:

> Translation is an operation performed on languages: a process of substituting a text in one language for a text in another. Clearly, then, any theory of translation must draw upon a theory of language—a general linguistic theory.[10]

If language has been described by linguists as "Patterned behaviour," the translation is an operation performed on two languages: the Source Language (SL) and the Target Language (TL). Translation is a transference of meaning from the Source Language (SL) to the Target Language (TL). Since meaning is the main goal in translation, there is not much difficulty in non-literary translation. But the difficulty arises when we are engaged in translation of literature. It is not easy to find the equivalent textual and literary material of the Source Language (SL) in the Target Language (TL).

Referring to the theory of translation Henry Mechonnic observes:

> It is a new field in the theory and in the practice of literature. Its epistemological importance lies in its contribution to the 'theoretical practice' of homogeneity of the natural union between the signifier and the signified. This homogenity is proper to that social enterprise which we call writing.[11]

Thus the problems of translation are greatly enhanced by linguistic indeterminacy which is the result of perpetual change. Next to it is the uncertainty of knowing the meaning of the 'text' accurately. In literature translation the 'text' is vital for it is the 'text' that has to be rendered into another language. The indeterminacy of a text is a crucial concept in contemporary literary criticism. Roland Barthes rightly observes that, 'as a limiting case, an ideal text that is infinitely plural and contrasts it with the classical text (*i.e.*, text classique), which is characterized by a limited or parsimonious plurality of sense.'[12] The author-text-reader triangle has undergone several changes in recent times. At one end stands the text created by the author and at the other stands the reader who experiences it. The text controls the reader's response, while the reader lends his own complexion to the text. Rajnath is right when he says that 'out of the interaction between the text and the reader comes into existence the literary construct.'[13] Wolfgang Iser maintains that "any description of the interaction between the two (text and the reader), must therefore incorporate both the structure of effects (the text) and that of response (the reader)."[14] Thus there are two 'texts' now: one the author's and another the reader's. "Text" is not what the author thought it to be but what the reader sees in it. Hence, the reader or the critic is the co-author and criticism is not an interpretation of the 'text' but an extension of it. Thus in such a state, what is the role of a translator and what will happen to translation? In addition to this there is the problem of the use of language in literature. If literary language is metaphorical, then which meaning should a translator take in translation—literal or metaphorical?

'In a translation process,' says A.K. Srivastava, "it is the metaphoric *metier* that provokes the problem of ambiguity even when assuming that the 'core' meaning arrived at by the translation represents the temper and tone of the original faithfully."[15] According to Professor Wheelwright "literature uses 'tensile' as opposed to 'Steno-language.'"[16] Literature expresses not one but several layers of meaning and in the words of Owen Barfield the ambiguity in literature "is the outcome of metaphoric organisation where the 'vehicle' may be fixed but the 'tenor' is polysemous."[17]

Robert Frost has once said that poetry is what is lost in translation but now critics say that poetry is lost in the very act of creation. Thus the function of deconstruction is not to deconstruct a text but to demonstrate how the text has deconstructed itself. But how to draw a line between the text deconstructing itself and the critic deconstructing the text? According to Derrida, '...the writer writes in a language and in a language whose proper system, laws and life his discourse by definition cannot dominate absolutely. He uses them only by letting himself after a fashion and upto a point, be governed by the system. And reading must always aim at a certain relationship unperceived by the Writer, between what he commands and what he does not command of the patterns of the language he uses....'[18] This means that the text has some patterns of language that has not been faithfully adhered to by the author.

The text according to structuralist and post-structuralist theories is no longer a writer's text but a reader's text, the product of the reader's act of reading (cf. W. Iser's *Act of Reading,* R. Barthes' *The Pleasure of the Text*) which goes on presenting a new text with each successive act of reading. Julia Kristeva finds this process of decoding as a semistic process that makes all texts translations of translations. The translator as he reads the text over again can produce another translation and as such reading itself becomes a translation. "The text becomes labyrinthine and translation a kin to her Menautics. As such as we move from the traditional definition of translation as the process of replacement of the text in SL by a text in TL for Maximum equivalence of meaning to the modem definition which stresses the process of transfer of a message from SL to TL, we encounter the problem of one or several levels of content of the message,"[19] says B. Das. Jakobson therefore regards translation as the interpretation of verbal signs by means of some other language. As such neither the SL text nor the TL text becomes stable.

Some traditional translation theorists divide translation into two types: literary and non-literary. In literary translation (*i.e.* translation of literature) the rhetoric of the Source Language (SL) should be faithfully carried over to the Target Language (TL). As G.E. Wellworth rightly suggested that in a literary translation, "what is required is the re-creation of a situation of cohesive semantic block in the new language in terms of the cultural setting of that language."[20] In other words, while translating a literary text, the translator decodes the motive of the text in the Source Language (SL) and re-encodes it in the translation.

As Susan Bassnett-McGuire rightly observes that "Translation involves for more than replacement of lexical and grammatical items between languages and as can be seen in the translation of idioms and metaphors, the process may involve discarding the basic linguistic elements of the SL text so as to achieve Popovic's goal of 'expressive identity' between the SL and TL texts. But once the translator moves away from close linguistic equivalence, the problems of determining the exact nature of the level of equivalence aimed for begin to emerge."[21]

What then, are the problems of translation? Ages ago Cicero summed up the translator's dilemma in the following words:

> If I render word for word, the result will sound uncouth and if compelled by necessity I alter anything in the order or wording. I shall seem to have departed from the function of a translator.[22]

A translator, in the first place, should possess an inwardness with both the languages—the source language (SL), from which the translation is to be made, and the target language (TL) into which the translation is to be done. He should have a mastery over both languages and the words should "obey his call." Above all, he should have the "feel" of the language. Secondly, in case of literature translation, literal translation should be avoided at all costs because it fails to carry the transposition of culture. The translator should not only give the lexical equivalent of words but keep in mind the socio-cultural matrix. Language is never a mechanical sound system, for each word is charged with memory, associations and literary allusions. Meenakshi Mukherjee makes an apt observation on this subject: (i) According to her, "the act of translation is voluntary, that is the material has been chosen by the translator himself and the prime mover is a compelling desire to recreate, (ii) The translator is a writer in the language in which he is translating, that is, his handling of the language is not merely competent but creative." Since language is to some extent culture oriented, translators face the problem of translating certain culture-based words into another language with a different culture. For instance, Lord Krishna's "Rasa Krida" is difficult to translate into English. Similarly, the translation of "Love Play" for "Lila" seems to me inadequate and something is missing in such a translation. For example, a word like "abhimana" has no equivalent word in English and "Pique" is a poor translation of that great word which has a lot of associations in Indian context. Moreover, Indian languages (particularly, Sanskrit) are rich in erotic vocabulary, but English language with all its richness and luxury is very poor in erotic vocabulary. Thus, the translation of Vatsyayan's *Kamasutra* into English fails to carry the "feel" of original writing with it. Moreover, words like "uncle," "aunt," "brother-in-law," "cousin" have a lot of equivalent words in Indian languages. How can one translate these culture-based words and "swear words" without taking the context and the "whole" into consideration?

The translator has to make a balance between maintaining close fidelity to the original and utter freedom from it. Sri Aurobindo is in favour of taking liberty with the original. He states that "a translator is not necessarily bound to the original he chooses; he can make his own poem out of it, if he likes, and that is what is generally done."[23] Translation is neither "transliteration" nor "transcreation" and it has to guard against the danger of word for word literal translation as well as taking too much liberty. In the name of creation in the light of recent literary criticism which holds indeterminacy of meaning as its central concept, the art of translation has become increasingly difficult. If each word is a sign and each sign has a signifier and a signified and again a signified is also a signifier then which meaning should one take in translation? Should one take the signification (linguistic code) of a word or its value into consideration for translation?

The importance of translation lies in the fact that it brings the readers, writers and critics of one nation into contact with those of others not only in the field of literature alone but in all areas of development: science and medicine, philosophy and religion, political science and medicine, and law and so on. Thus translation helps in the cause of nation building.

In the Indian context the translator has a greater role to play. Several regional literatures of the country can reach all the Indian readers only through translation. So to say, India is a Paradise for translators and translation has a great scope in our country. Translation in the modern context is not secondary to original literature in the source language. It is not reproduction but recreation. It has become "new literature" may be "literature three" if you will, thanks to the recent discoveries in the field of linguistics and literary criticism. With the "indeterminacy of meaning" of a "text," the need for translation in the Modern World is now greater than ever before.

## NOTES


1. Krishnaswamy, et al., *Modern Applied Linguistics* (Madras: MacMillan, 1992) 235.
2. A.H. Smith, ed., *Aspects of Translation* (London: Seeker and Warburg, 1988) 8.
3. J.C. Catford, *A Linguistic Theory of Translation* (London: OUP, 1965) 20.
4. *Ibid.*, 21.
5. R.S. Pathak (Quoted), "Untranslatability: Myth or Reality," *Critical Practice* 1: 2 (1994).
6. Theodore Savory, *The Art of Translation* (London: Cape, 1957).
7. Eric Jacobsen, *Translation: A Traditional Craft* (Copenhagen: Nordisk Forlag, 1958).
8. Eugene Nida, *Towards a Science of Translating* (Leiden: E.J. Brill, 1964).
9. Horst Frenz, "The Art of Translation" in N.P. Stallknecht and H. Frenz (eds.), *Comparative Literature: Method and Perspective* (Carbondale: South Illinois University Press, 1961) 72-96.
10. Catford, 1.
11. George Steiner, "Epigraph," *After Babel* (Oxford, 1975).
12. Roland Barthes, "Sign, Sense and Roland" in *Literary Criticism: Idea and Act* (Berkeley: University of California Press, 1974) 235.
13. Rajnath, "The Text and the Reader: A Critique of Reader Response Criticism," *Journal of Literary Criticism* 3: 1 (1986) 19.
14. Wolfgang Iser, *The Act of Reading* (Baltimore: The John Hopkins University Press, 1980) 21.
15. A.K. Srivastava, "On Translating Literature," *The Literary Criterion* 22: 2 (1987) 19.
16. Philip Wheelwright, *The Burning Fountain: A Study in the Language of Symbolism*, Bloomington, 1954.
17. Owen Barfield, "Imagination and Inspiration" in *Interpretation: The Poetry of Meaning* (ed.), Hopper and Miller.
18. Jonathan Culler (Quoted), "Jacques Derrida," *Structuralism and Since,* 173.
19. Bidhubhusan Das, "Some Criteria of Acceptability in Translation," *Journal of Literary Studies* 13: 2 (1989) 29-30.
20. G.E. Wellworth, "Special Considerations in Drama Translation," *Translation Spectrum: Essays in Theory and Practice,* ed. M.G. Rox (New York, 1987) 143.

21. Susan Bassnett-McGuire, *Translation Studies* (London: Routledge, 1991) 25.
22. *Ibid.*, 43.
23. Prema Nandakumar (Quoted), "Translation: A Creative Process," *Cygnus* 2: 2, 65.

# 2

# The Diachronic Study of Translation

Translation studies in our time has acquired a new dimension—thanks to the development in the field of linguistics. But no study of Translation can be proper and appropriate without making a reference to the background or history of it. Translation studies from the Roman system to the closing decades of the twentieth century have undergone several changes. In order to examine the aspects of Translation in their proper perspective, it is imperative on our part to have a look at the background of Translation studies in the West when the translators first began to translate following the Roman system.

Translation has been regarded as a secondary activity as a 'mechanical' rather than a 'creative' process, and therefore, considered lower in status. Hilaire Belloc summed up the problem of status in his Taylorian Lecture on Translation in 1931:

> The art of translation is a subsidiary art and derivative. On this account it has never been granted the dignity of original work, and has suffered too much in the general judgement of letters. This natural underestimation of its value has had the bad practical effect of lowering the standard demanded and in some periods has almost destroyed the art altogether. The corresponding misunderstanding of its character has added to its degradation: neither its importance nor its difficulty has been grasped.[1] (qtd. in Bassnett-McGuire 2)

In the western metaphysics translation is an exile and in the words of J. Hills Miller, "Translation is the wandering existence in a perpetual exile"[2] (qtd. in Devy 135). A French translator, namely Etienne Dolet (1509-46) was executed for attempting a rather 'free' translation of Plato. G.N. Devy gives an interesting account of the origin and development of the art of translation in the West in the following lines:

> Translation was heresy and protest not only during the Renaissance Europe. It was probably, so for the first great philosopher of Europe, Plato. The Platonic objection to poetry was that it distorts reality while it translates things into verbal forms. As against him Aristotle upheld the honour of poetry by saying that while it imitates reality it does create aesthetically pleasing structures. Mimesis a pre-linguistic translation in Jakobson's view did remain the central concept in his philosophy of creativity. Translation indeed is the crucial metaphor for creativity in western literary thought. In times of profound social changes Europe had often renewed its creativity by restoring to translation, by returning the metaphor to its origin of literality. The English and German translation of the *Bible* (King James' Version and Martin Luther's Version), which enriched these two languages so substantially, were such attempts. Interestingly, modern Europe's celebration of its modernity through these acts of translation conceded with its attempt to humanise and internalise the myth of 'perpetual exile'. Translation is at once a move away from the original and an effort to re-situate the original. To the western consciousness it is a paradox.[3]

The distinction between 'word for word' and 'sense for sense' translation, established within the Roman system still continues to a point of debate among scholars and translators of our time. Close to this, the persecution of Bible translators during the centuries when scholars were avidly translating and re-translating classical Greek and Roman authors still rings in our ears. Notwithstanding the distance that separates us in the twentieth century from the Bible translators of the past scholars have made an attempt to trace the growth and development of translation in terms of periods. The most significant of them is George Steiner who in After Babel[4] divided "the literature on theory, practice and history of translation into four periods," says McGuire (40).

She further writes: "According to Steiner, the first period begins from the statements of Cicero and Horace on translation and ends with the Publication of A.F. Tytler's *Essay on the Principles of Translation* in 1791". The chief characteristic of this period is that of 'immediate empirical focus,' *i.e.*, the theories and statements about translation come directly from the practical work of translating. The second period, according to him, which lasts till 1946, is characterized as a period of 'theory and hermeneutic enquiry with the development of a vocabulary and methodology of approaching translation.' The third period commences with the publication of the first papers on machine translation in the 1940s and is marked by the introduction of structural linguistics and communication theory into translation's study. And the fourth period which coexists with the third has its origins in the early 1960s and is marked by 'a reversion to hermeneutic, almost metaphysical inquiries into translation and interpretation,' in brief by a vision which sets 'translation in a wide frame that includes a number of other disciplines': "Classical philology and comparative literature, lexical statistics and ethnography, the sociology of class speech, formal rhetoric, poetics and the study of grammar are combined in an attempt to clarify the act of translation and the process of 'life between languages.'"[5]

This periodization of translation studies is not acceptable to many. Susan Bassnett-McGuire differs from Steiner on the question of division of literature into periods on the basis of translation and states her views in the following words:

> It is virtually impossible to divide periods according to dates for, as Lotman points out, human culture is a dynamic system. Attempts to locate stages of cultural development within strict temporal boundaries contradict that dynamism. A splendid example of the kind of difficulties that arise from the 'periodization approach' emerge when we consider the problem of defining the temporal limits of the Renaissance. There is a large body of literature that attempts to decide whether Petrarch and Chaucer were medieval or Renaissance writers, whether Rabelais was a medieval mind 'post hoc' or whether Dante was a Renaissance mind two centuries too

> soon. An examination of translation in those terms would not be very helpful at all.[6]

In spite of the debates over the division of translation as a study into periods some concepts of translation at different times can be recorded. For example, T.R. Steiner examines the theory of translation "between the cut-off dates of 1650-1800, which starts with Sir John Denham and ends with William Cowper, and analyses the eighteenth century idea of the translator as painter or imitator. Andre Lefevere's document of translation traces the establishment of a German tradition of translation, which starts with Luther and ends with Rosenzweig. F.O. Mattiesson analyses the four major English translators of the sixteenth century (though not very systematically) within a particular time frame. These four translators are Hoby, North, Florio, and Philemon Holland" (Bassnett-McGuire 41). Timothy Webb's methodology "involves a careful analysis of the work of an individual translator in relation to the rest of his opus and to contemporary concepts of the role and status of translation."[7]

The study of 'translation' periodwise may be debated but its value for the growth of literature in a language and in a country is beyond question. That is why, in spite of a number of critical statements about the value of translation in the development of the Roman literary rule, the need for a planned study of Roman translation theory in English seems to be urgent. And rightly Susan Bassnett-McGuire contests Mattiesson's claim when the latter declared that "a study of Elizabethan translations is a study of the means by which the Renaissance came to England."[8] McGuire elaborates in the following words:

> In trying to establish certain lines of approach to translation, across a time period that extends from Cicero to the present, it seems best to proceed by following a loosely chronological structure, but without making any attempt to set up clear cut divisions. Hence, instead of trying to talk in what must inevitably be very general terms about a specifically 'Renaissance' or 'classical' concept of translation, I have tried to follow lines of approach that may or may not be easily locatable in a temporal context. So the Word for

Word Vs. Sense for Sense lines can be seen emerging again and again with different concepts of language and communication.[9]

The history of Translation Studies in the West begins with the Romans. Eric Jacobsen, maintains in the book, *Translation, A Traditional Craft* that translation is a Roman invention, and this view serves as a starting point from which attention on the role and status of translation for the Romans can be focused. The opinions of both Cicero and Horace on translation had a great influence on successive translators. Both discuss translation according to the two main functions of the poet; the universal human duty of gaining and diffusing wisdom and the special art of making and shaping a poem.

The value of translation in the literature of Rome has been used to blame the Romans of being unable to produce imaginative literature in their own right, at least until the first century B.C. With translation there is the text of the source language (SL) to be imitated and not to be crushed by the strict application of Reason. Cicero expresses this distinction: "If I render word for word, the result will sound uncouth, and if compelled by necessity I alter anything in the order or wording, I shall seem to have departed from the function of a translator."[10]

But Cicero and Horace make a distinction between 'word for word' translation and 'sense for sense' translation. According to the Roman notion, the process of enrichment of the literary system is an important part of translation and there is a concern for language enrichment also. Both Horace and Cicero view that the art of the translator should be the judicious interpretation of the text of the source language (SL) so as to create a version of the target language (TL) based on the rule of expressing not word for word, but sense for sense and his responsibility was to the readers of the target languages (TL).

But there is also an extra aspect of the Roman idea of enrichment through translation, *i.e.,* the pre-eminence of Greek as the cultural language and the ability of educated Romans to read the source language texts. The position of both the translator and the reader changes when these factors are accounted.

Translation was regarded as a meta text in relation to the original by the Roman readers. So Roman translation may be considered as unique because it springs from a vision of literary production that follows an established rule of excellence across linguistic boundaries.

"With the spread of Christianity, translation came to acquire another role that of disseminating the word of God,"[11] says McGuire. The history of *Bible* translation may be considered as the Western culture's history in microcosm. If translation may be taken as a metaphysical riddle, yet it is a mighty political weapon. It is a way of applying power to oneself. *The Bible* translations were neither literary exercises, nor spiritual enterprises, they were clearly meant for political defence. *The Bible* translation across the world was motivated by missionary activity to spread the Christian religion. Thus the translations of the *Bible* became a hot bed of debate upto the seventeenth century, and the problems increased with the growth of ideas of national culture and with the coming of the reformation. Translation was used as an instrument of defence in both dogmatic and political conflicts with the rise of nation states and the decline of the Church's influence. The Wycliffite *Bible* translated between 1380 and 1384 was the first rendering of the complete *Bible* into English. It marked the beginning of a great flowering of English translations of *Bible* linked to changing conditions to the role of the written text in the Church, that constituted part of the developing reformation.

The history of the translation of the *Bible* is in fact the history of the translation studies in the West in the sixteenth century. The translators of the *Bible* during the Renaissance period saw both fluidity and intelligibility in the next of the target language (TL) as important criteria, but were equally engaged with the transmission of literary accurate message. In the sixteenth century the *Bible* was translated into a large number of European languages.

Several theoreticians and translators such as Quintilian (Roman theoretician of first century A.D.), Gianfranco Folena, Roger Bacon, Dante and others have their own views of translation. For Quintilian translation was a stylistic exercise, and to Alfred translation involved the creation of a vernacular SL text. Gianfranco Folena suggested that medieval translation might be described either as vertical or horizontal. By vertical translation he meant the translation into the vernacular from an SL (source language) that had a special prestige and to him in horizontal translation both SL and TL (target language) had a similar value. Both Roger Bacon and Dante spoke of translation in relation to the moral and aesthetic criteria of works of art. I am inclined to agree with Susan Bassnett-McGuire who has neatly presented a balanced view of translation after carefully examining others' views of it:

> The distinction between horizontal and vertical translation is helpful in that it shows how translation could be linked to two coexistent but different literary systems. However, there are many different strands in the development of literary translation upto the early fifteenth century and Folena's distinction only sheds light on one small area. And whilst the vertical approach splits into two distinct types, the interlinear gloss, or word-for-word technique, as opposed to the Ciceronian sense-for-sense method, elaborated by Quintilian's concept of paraphrase, the 'horizontal' approach involves complex questions of 'imitation' and borrowing. The high status of 'imitation' in the medieval canon meant that originality of material was not greatly prized and an author's skill consisted in the reworking of established themes and ideas. The point at which a writer considered himself to be a translator of another text, as opposed to the use he might make of translated material plagiarized from other texts, is rarely clear. Within the opus of a single writer, such as Chaucer (c. 1340-1400) there is a range of texts that include acknowledged translations, free adaptations, conscious borrowings, reworkings and close correspondences. And although theoreticians such as Dante or John of Trevisa (1326-1412) raise the question of accuracy in translation, that notion of accuracy is dependent on the translator's ability to read and understand the original and does not rest on the translator's subordination to that SL text. Translation, whether vertical or horizontal, is viewed as a skill, inextricably

bound up with modes of reading and interpreting the original text, which is proper source material for the writer to draw upon as he thinks fit.[12]

The role of translation underwent important changes after the invention of printing methods in the fifteenth century. During this time, attempts were made to form a theory of translation. Dolet, a French humanist outlined the translation theory in the following words:

(1) The translator must fully understand the sense and meaning of the original author, although he is at liberty to clarify obscurities.

(2) The translator should have a perfect knowledge of both SL and TL.

(3) The translator should avoid word for word renderings.

(4) The translator should use forms of speech in common use.

(5) The translator should choose and order words appropriately to produce the correct tone.[13]

Dolet's principles (*i.e.*, the theory of translation) lay stress on the importance of the understanding of the SL text as the first requisite. He is of the opinion that a translator is or ought to be far more competent than a linguist. He holds the view that "translation involves a scholarly and sensitive appraisal of the SL text," so that the TL text would not be far removed from it.

During the Renaissance, in Europe, translation formed a logic of relation between past and present, and between distinct tongues and traditions which were divided under pressure of nationalism and religious conflict.

The role of translation changed by the mid-seventeenth century. Denham speaks in favour of a notion that perceives translator and original writer as equal though they work in clearly distinct social and temporal contexts. He views that it is the translator's faithfulness to his source text to extract what he sees as the essential core of the work and to reproduce or recreate the work in the target language.

In his Preface to *Ovid's Epistles* (1680), Dryden formulated three basic types of translation to tackle the problems of translations:

(i) 'metaphrase' or turning an author word by word, and line by line, from one language into another.

(ii) 'paraphrase' or translation with latitude, the Ciceronian 'sense-for-sense' view of translation.

(iii) 'imitation,' where the translator can abandon the text of the original as he sees fit.[14]

Dryden prefers the second category to the other two for he considers it a balanced path. He says that for translating poetry, the translator should be a poet, should be a master of both the languages and should comprehend the 'spirit' of the original writer and conform to the aesthetic laws of his own age. He compares the translator with the portrait-painter, maintaining that the duty of the painter is to make his portrait resemble the original. The views of Dryden on translation was supported by Alexander Pope, who spoke of the same moderate path as Dryden, with emphasis on close reading of the original to mark the details of style and manner while trying to keep alive the 'fire' of the poem. The history of translation from the translation of the *Bible* from Wycliffe to the Authorised Version to Dryden and Pope belies Hilaire Belloc's view (Quoted in the beginning of this chapter) that translation is subsidiary and derivative.

The idea of Dryden and Pope of translation is an important factor, beyond the problem of the debate between "over-faithfulness and looseness." The whole question of the translator's responsibility to his contemporary reader is mind boggling. The motive to make clear the essential 'spirit' of a text led to a number of re-writings of earlier texts to make them suitable to contemporary criteria of language and taste. So the texts of Shakespeare were re-structured and the works of Racine were translated. Dr. Johnson analysing the question of additions to a text through translation, remarks that "if elegance is gained," and nothing is taken away, then it is desirable and further states that 'the purpose of the writer is to be read.' The claim of the man to be addressed in his own words, on his own ground is a significant factor in the translation of the eighteenth century and is connected to changing ideas or 'originality.'

The eighteenth century comparison of the translator with painter or imitator with his moral duty both to the original subject and to the receiver was well-known. But it had undergone a series of important alterations as the search to codify and describe the modes of literary creation changed. Goethe remarks that every literature must pass through three modes of translation, although all the modes may be found taking place within the same language system at the same time. The first phase makes us familiar 'with foreign countries on our own terms.' The second phase makes the translator absorb the sense of a foreign work but reproduces it in his words. The aim of the third phase is perfect identity between the text of the source language and the text of the target language and the performing of this phase must be through the creation of a new 'manner' which melts "the uniqueness of the original with a new form and structure." This mode is regarded as the highest by Goethe.

Towards the close of the eighteenth century, Alexander Fraser Tytler published a volume titled, *The Principles of Translation* in 1791, the first systematic study of the translation process in English and laid down three basic principles:

(i) The translation should give a complete transcript of the idea of the original work.

(ii) The style and manner of writing should be of the same character with that of the original work.

(iii) The translation should have all the ease of the original composition.[15]

Tytler takes Dryden, to task for the concept of 'paraphrase' that led to immoderately loose translations, although he agrees that part of the duty of the translator is to make clear that obscurities in the original, even where this entails omission or addition. He accepts the eighteenth century comparison of the translator with the painter, but with a difference, that is, the translator cannot use the same colours as the original. However, the translator is supposed to give his picture the same force and effect. The translator must try to take the author's soul, which must speak through his own organs.

The theory of translation from Dryden to Tytler, then is beset with the problem of recreating an essential spirit and nature of the work of art.

The distinctions made by Goethe among types of translation and stages in a hierarchy of aesthetic evaluation is a sign of a shift in attitude to translation resulting from a revaluation of the role of poetry and creativity. During the Romantic period, the ambiguous attitude of a number of major writers and translators can be seen in the discussion on the nature of translation. A.W. Schlegel, while declaring that all acts of speaking and writing are translations because the nature of communication is to decode and interpret messages received, also demanded that the original form should be kept. Meanwhile, Friedrich Schlegel imagined of translations as a class of thought rather than as an activity concerned with language or literature. Emphasis on the effect of the translation in the target culture in fact resulted in a change of interest away from the actual methods of translation. Moreover, two conflicting attitudes can be seen in the early part of the nineteenth century. One accepts translation as a class of thought, with the translator perceived as a creative genius in his own right, and enriching the literature and language into which he is translating. The other thinks of translation with its mechanical function of 'making known' a text or author. The pre-eminence of Imagination assumes that translation must be inspired by the higher creative force to be more than an activity of the everyday world with the loss of the original shaping spirit. Shelley regarded translation as a lower activity, as a method of filling the gaps between the inspirations. Shelley seems to change from translating works praised for their concepts to translating works appreciated for their literary grace. This change is important, because it follows the hierarchy in translating advocated by Goethe and it shows the problems which translation made in the formulation of a Romantic aesthetic. The idea that meaning lies below and between language created a deadlock for the translator. Comparing the two period of translations, G.N. Devy observes: "While the Renaissance translations were attempts to raise the status of the translators' culture, the Romantic translations were aimed at raising the culture status of the works translated."[16]

In the post-Romantic period Friedrich Schleiermacher advocated the cause of the creation of distinct sub-language for use in translated literature only, when D.G. Rossetti declared the subservience of the translator to the forms and language of the original. The theory of a distinct translation language by Friedrich was shared by many English translators of nineteenth century like Newman, Carlyle and William Morris, Newman remarked that the translator should keep every peculiar quality of the original.

Matthew Arnold advises the common reader to trust the scholars, for they alone can tell whether the translation produces more or less the same impact as the original. In his first lecture on Translating Homer, he advised the would be translators in the following words:

> Let not the translator, then, trust to his notions of what the ancient Greeks would have thought of him; he will lose himself in vague. Let him not trust to what the ordinary English reader thinks of him; he will be taking the blind for his guide. Let him not trust to his own judgement of his own work. He may be misled by individual caprices. Let him ask how his work affects those who both know Greek and can appreciate poetry.[17]

Arnold is of the opinion that the primary duty of the translator is to focus on the text of the source language, so that he can serve that text with complete commitment. The reader of the target language must be brought to the text of the source language through translation, a condition that is the opposite of the expression given by Erasmus, when analysing the need for accessibility of the text of the source language. And with the hardening of nationalistic lines and growth of national culture's pride, French, English or German translators, for instance no longer viewed translation as an elementary way of enriching their own culture. If translation was seen as an instrument, as a way of bringing the reader of the target language to the text of the source language, then the excellence of style and the ability of the translator to write were of less significance. H.W. Longfellow added another dimension to translation by outlining the business of a translator:

> The business of a translator is to report what the author says, not to explain what he means; that is the work of the commentator. What an author says and how he says it, that is the problem of the translator?[18]

The translator is consigned to the position of a technician, neither poet nor commentator, with a defined but strictly limited task. The business of the translator is to report what the author says but not what he means.

Contrasting with the views of Longfellow, Edward Fitzgerald, stated that a text must live at all costs with a transfusion of one's own worst life if one cannot maintain the better of the original. The work of Edward does not try to lead the reader of the target language to the original source language, instead it tries to bring a version of the text of the source language into the culture of the target language as a living entity, though his some what extreme opinion on the lowliness of the text of the source language, shows a patronizing attitude that demonstrates another form of 'elitism'. According to Romantic individualist tradition, the translator is seen as a skilful trader giving exotic wares to the discerning few.

McGuire classifies the main trends of translation typology in the age of industrial capitalism and colonial expansion up to the First World War in the following words:

(1) Translation as a scholar's activity, where the pre-eminence of the SL text is assumed *de facto* over any TL version.

(2) Translation as a means of encouraging the intelligent reader to return to the SL original.

(3) Translation as a means of helping the TL reader become the equal of what Schleiermacher called the better reader of the original, through a deliberately contrived foreignness in the TL text.

(4) Translation as a means whereby the individual translator who sees himself like Aladdin in the enchanted vaults

(Rosserti's imaginative image) offers his own pragmatic choice to the TL reader.

(5) Translation as a means through which the translator seeks to upgrade the status of the SL text because it is perceived as being on a lower cultural level.[19]

McGuire's classification opens up the possibility of both 'literal' and 'free' translation. Hence, it is upto the translator to stick to any kind of transaction.

The theory and practice of translation in the first half of the twentieth century are in continuation with the Victorian ideas of translation—literalness, archaizing and pedantry. Ezra Pound's work is of great significance in the history of translation and the skill of Pound as a translator was a suitable match to his perceptiveness as critic and theorist.

The Western concept of translation and translator has undergone several changes in the last three centuries. This is due to the changes in the cultural history of the West. The view of the translator as a shadowy presence by Steiner and the view of Larbaud on the translator as a beggar at the Church door, is necessarily a post-Romantic view and has something to do with ideas of hierarchy in the chain of communication between writer and text, translator and reader than with any intrinsic aspect of the process of translation. It is to be noted that the gestures towards translation and the ideas of translation that prevail, belong to the age that produces them, and to the socio-economic elements which shape that age.

The concept of translation has acquired a new dimension in the twentieth century—particularly with the emphasis on language and role of language in literature, given by the New Critics, Saussure, Levi-Strauss, Chomsky, Roland Barthes, Derrida and Foucault. Translation of literature is possible only because it is written in a language. (One cannot think of the translation of music, art, painting and architecture, as they are not based on language.) But no two languages function alike and that is why rendering an SL text into a TL text creates problems. For New Critics, 'text' is an autonomous unity and therefore, it becomes difficult to have an exact or accurate translation of the text.

Since no two readings are identical, no translator can claim to have perceived the author's meaning completely and accurately. The problem is how to get at the author's meaning.

The Structuralists believe that a work can be peeled off to express a void at centre and that makes translation difficult. Derrida and his followers have pleaded an absence of meaning. They say that words carry with them no definite meaning but they are characterized by an indeterminacy of meaning. Hence, the new theories of criticism have made the act of translation difficult. However, notwithstanding these difficulties, translation continues to flourish in our time.

After having discussed the history of translation in the West let us take a look at how translation flourished in India.

The political importance of translation can be seen in the tradition of India too. In India the Bhakti Movement of Poetry had the desire of translating the spiritual language from Sanskrit into the colloquial language. However, as a political weapon, translation is not always used for reducing the gap between the divine and the profane, the high and the low.

The modern languages of India have a long history of translations from Sanskrit as they are originated from Sanskrit. The literary traditions of these are full of examples of numerous renderings of the epics of Sanskrit and other literatures. In the beginning of the literary tradition many of the modern Indian languages have remarkable translations. *Jnanesvari* in Marathi may be taken as an example. These translations did not care to follow a word for word and line for line rule. The conditions necessary for the study of these translations are not the target language and the source language or the mother tongue and the other tongue. The poets or writers trying native translations of Sanskrit texts regarded both the languages as their 'own' languages. They had a possessive sense for the Sanskrit heritage. But in translating the Sanskrit texts they wanted to free the scriptures from the monopoly of limited class of people. So these translations aimed at re-organizing the society. No theory with a special linguistic orientation can be enough to grasp the total magnitude of this traditional Indian translation activity.

The colonialism of Britishers created a conflict in Indian cultural priorities. Thus a desire for fast westernization was produced. It also produced an inclination to awaken the culture of the past, much of it left behind in the natural course of time. Colonialism produced a desire for national unity in addition to these two inclinations. These three inclinations—"Westernization," "Revivalism," "Nationalism"—are suitably expressed in the translations of the colonial period in India.

There is a difference between the medieval translations from Sanskrit and the translations of the colonial period. The aim of the medieval translations was to free the society, whereas the translations of the colonial period were only 'reactionary.' They came either as a reaction to the colonial situation which shocked the Indian national pride, or as copies of the Indological translations of Sanskrit by scholars like Sir William Jones, Max Muller, etc. The cultural scene of India was changing very fast by the end of the First World War. After knowing the European cultures other than the British, a large number of soldiers of India returned home. The entrance of Mahatma Gandhi in the political scene of India also created a new national awareness. As a result of these changes, the translators of India now turned to European literature and the literature in other Indian languages. Thus, during the freedom struggle of India, interlingual exchange within Indian languages was increased. For instance, the works of Tagore, were translated into all Indian languages. Such were the cases of Premchand, K.M. Munshi and V.S. Khandekar.

The translation scene in India shows a new tendency during the post-colonial decades. Most Indian writers contend with each other to translate their works into English. So there is an increase in the number of translations from Indian languages into English. At present it has become a symbol of status for the Indian writers to translate their works into English.

From the above-mentioned facts it is clear that translation is not a politically innocent activity. The political motivations of translation may not be on the surface, but when it is considered within the entire cultural context, these motives can become clear. Therefore, translation is not only a linguistic activity but a cultural act. Due to this, the nature of translation theory cannot be universally uniform. The national and cultural past guides the translation work. Hence, the actual translation practice in a given culture and language is necessary for the formation of any theory of translation.

Great improvements have been made in Translation Studies since mid-sixties. It is searching thoroughly new ground and bridging the gap between the vast area of stylistics, literary history, linguistics, semiotics and aesthetics. But at the same time it is necessary to remember that as a discipline it is firmly rooted in practical application.

From the above discussion it appears that Translation Studies dates back to centuries of the past when both in the East and in the West, translators had made efforts to translate literary texts from one language into another. Translation continues to grow in spite of the new theories of language and the question of translatability of 'literary texts' raised by theoreticians in our time. The need for translation is greater than ever before in our time. This is because we live in multi-lingual and multi-cultural society where the need for interaction between people of different linguistic groups and cultures is highly necessary. Translation fulfils that goal of putting across the view of the people in a multi-lingual society. Thus, translation has acquired a place for itself in the highly-sophisticated techno-electronic age.

The diachronic study of translation reveals that there is a fundamental difference between Western and Eastern attitude to translation. When translation was considered as 'subsidiary and derivative' in the West, in the East it was traditionally considered as 'new writing.' The notion and anxiety of exactness or true to the original both in letter and spirit did not bother the Indian translators upto the nineteenth century. For example, Sanskrit epics and puranas continued to be adapted, retold and translated into several regional languages and were well received by the public. But the modern Indian translators being influenced by the Western counterparts insisted on exact equivalence and deviated from the path shown by their ancestors. Thus, in the second-half of the twentieth century, both Eastern and Western translators with their knowledge of linguistics and literary criticism have taken translation seriously—as an art, a craft and above all, a Science.

## NOTES

1. Hilaire Belloc, *On Translation* (Oxford: The Clarendon Press, 1931) qtd. in Susan Bassnett-McGuire, *Translation Studies.* London: Routledge, 1991.
2. G.N. Devy, quoted, "Translation Theory: An Indian Perspective," *In Another Tongue* (Madras: MacMillan India Ltd., 1993) 135.
3. G.N. Devy, "Translation Theory: An Indian Perspective," *Anuvada* 2.2 (1991): 5.
4. George Steiner, *After Babel* (London: Oxford University Press, 1975) 236.
5. Susan Bassnett-McGuire, quoted, *Translation Studies* (London: Routledge, 1991) 40.
6. *Ibid.*, 41.
7. *Ibid.*, 42.
8. *Ibid.*, 42.
9. *Ibid.*, 42.
10. *Ibid.* (Quoted) 43.
11. *Ibid.*, 45.
12. *Ibid.*, 53.
13. *Ibid.* (Quoted) 54.
14. *Ibid.* (Quoted) 60.
15. *Ibid.* (Quoted) 63.
16. Devy (1993) 137.
17. Matthew Arnold, "On Translating Homer," *Essays by Matthew Arnold* (London: Oxford University Press, 1914) 247.
18. Henry Wordsworth Longfellow, quoted in William J. De Sue, *Dante into English* (Chapel Hill: University of North Carolina Press, 1964) 65.
19. Bassnett-McGuire (1991) 71.

# 3

# Kinds of Translation

Traditional translation theorists divided translation into two types: literary and non-literary. In literary translation (*i.e.,* the translation of literature) the translators were concerned with both 'sense' and style. But in non-literary translation the emphasis was on sense. It was meant not to be 'word for word' but 'sense for sense' translation. In the later half of the twentieth century with the advent of Structuralism, Deconstruction and Reader-Response Criticism, Translation Studies took a new turn.

Apart from literary and non-literary translations, there are a number of other types of translation such as literal translation (which aims—to be basically "word for word"), Phonological translation [which is "restricted" translation where the phonology of the (SL) text is substituted by an equivalent phonology in the (TL) text], Graphological translation [which is "restricted" translation where the graphology of the (SL) text is substituted by equivalent graphology in the (TL) text], and Grammatical translation (which is "restricted" translation where the grammar of the source language text is substituted by equivalent grammar in the target language but the lexis is not replaced). In recent years translators taking a cue from the linguists and literary critics have extended the meaning and significance of translation by attempting at different kinds of translation, such as "phonological," "graphological," "total," "restricted," "full," "partial," "rank-bound," "free," "literal," "transliteration" and "transcription", etc.

As pointed out above, in the past there was a debate among scholars on the nature of translation. Some favoured 'word for word' translation as against 'sense for sense' translation of others. Some scholars even advocated transmission of sense across the language. Both Horace and Cicero made a distinction between 'word for word' and 'sense for sense' translation. What is desired in translation is not so much a translation of words but a translation of meanings.

John Dryden divided translation into three basic types. In the preface to *Ovid's Epistles* (1680) he categorized the problems of translation by formulating them as follows:

(1) metaphrase, or turning an author word by word and line by line, from one language into another.

(2) paraphrase, or translation with latitude, the Ciceronian 'sense for sense' view of translation.

(3) imitation, where the translator can abandon the text of the original as he sees fit.[1]

In the translation of literature or a literary text, the translator has to bear in mind the basic principles of literature. That is, literature being a skilled subject does not give definite answer to a question. What I want to say is that in literature there is no 'yes' and 'no' type of answer and instead, there is a variety of approach to study a literary text. Moreover, the language of literature being metaphorical (or rhetorical), the translator should try to create an appropriate rhetoric in TL text while translating an SL text. In other words, the TL text must retain the 'feel' of the original SL text.

According to G.E. Wellworth, in a literary translation, "what is required is the re-creation of a situation or cohesive semantic block in the new language in terms of the cultural setting of that language."[2] In literary translation, the translator decodes the motive of the SL text and re-encodes it in the TL text. In other words, an SL text gets recontextualized in the TL text. That is why Chandra Sekhar Patil calls literary translation 'a transplantation of experience'[3] from one linguistic plain to another. In literary translation the mode of displacement continues. That is why literary translation is considered as a method of 'avant-garde writing.'

The non-literary translation takes place in the realms of Physical Science, Social Science, Journalism, Law, etc. In these disciplines and subjects a definite question has a definite answer. Here we are concerned with the 'meanings' but not with the style. In non-literary translation content gets precedence over form. Therefore, while translating political, scientific, economic theories from SL to TL the translator is concerned with the transference of meaning. The same is the case with journalistic articles.

Translation being a communicative activity, must be studied both as a product and a process from the semiotic point of view. Since language and culture are interlinked, no literary text can be treated in isolation from the culture to which it belongs and again, of which it is a product. Roman Jakobson divides translation into the following types:

(1) Intralingual translation: which is an interpretation of verbal signs by means of other signs in the same system.

(2) Interlingual translation or translation proper: this is interpretation of verbal signs by means of verbal signs in some other linguistic system.

(3) Intersemiotic translation or transmutation: this is an interpretation of verbal signs by means of signs of non-verbal sign systems.[4]

The Intralingual translation of a word uses either another more or less synonymous word or resorts to a circumlocution (or Periphrasis). And yet synonymy, as a rule, is not complete equivalence: for example, 'every celibate is a bachelor, but not every bachelor is a celibate.' A word or an idiomatic phrase-word, briefly a code-unit of the highest level, may be fully interpreted only by means of an equivalent combination of code units; *i.e.,* a message referring to this code-unit: 'every bachelor is an unmarried man, and every unmarried man is a bachelor,' or 'every celibate is bound not to marry, and everyone who is bound not to marry is a celibate.'

But no full equivalence is possible through translation. Jakobson rightly observes: "likewise, on the level of interlingual translation, there is ordinarily no full equivalence between code-units, while messages may serve as adequate interpretations of alien code-units or messages."[5] It is common knowledge that every synonymy does not produce equivalence and Jakobson states that intralingual translation resorts to code units to interpret the meaning of a single unit. So 'perfect' may be taken as the synonym for 'ideal' or 'conveyance' may be synonymous with 'vehicle' but in neither case it would be complete equivalence, because each unit contains within itself a set of non-transferable associations and connotations. Hence, Jakobson maintains that all poetic art is technically untranslatable as complete equivalence is not possible in any of his types.

Jakobson's approach makes it clear that no translation however accurate it may be can provide the exact equivalence of the messages of the SL text in the TL text. Hence, the central problem for the translator is to establish equivalence between the SL text and the TL text. It is argued (and rightly so) that all types of translation involve these three, *i.e.*, loss of meaning, addition of meaning, and finally, skewing of meaning. Hence, total translation is a myth. The translator becomes the 'de-coder' of the SL text and 're-coder' of the TL text. And between 'de-coding' and 're-coding' falls the shadow.

Apart from literary and non-literary translation, there can be 'total' and 'restricted translation' or 'full' and 'partial' translation. J.C. Catford makes a classification of translation in terms of extent, level and ranks. The destination between 'full' and 'partial' translation is made in terms of extent. In a 'full' translation, every part of the SL text is replaced by the material in the TL text. As Catford says:

> In a partial translation, some part or parts of the SL text are left untranslated: they are simply transferred to and incorporated in the TL text. In literary translation it is not uncommon for some SL lexical items to be treated in this way, either because they are regarded as 'untranslatable' or for the deliberate purpose of introducing 'local colour' into the TL text. This process of transferring SL lexical items into a TL text is more complex than appears at first sight, and it is only approximately true to say that they remain

untranslated. The distinction between 'full' and 'partial' translation is not technical.[6]

Catford makes a distinction between 'total' and 'restricted' translation which is related to the levels of language in translation. He defines 'total' translation as "replacement of SL grammar and lexis by equivalent TL grammar and lexis with consequential replacement of SL phonology/graphology by (non-equivalent) TL phonology/graphology."[7] A restricted translation is that where the SL textual material is replaced by equivalent TL textual material at one level only.

Catford further suggests another type of equivalence in translation which connects the rank in a grammatical hierarchy with the translation formed. This is called 'rank-bound' translation. In 'rank-bound' translation, the selection of TL equivalents is made at the same rank. A 'word-rank-bound' translation is necessary for showing the differences between the source language and the target language in the construction of higher-rank units. The 'rank-bound' translation is often considered as bad translation, because it uses TL equivalents which are not proper to their position in the text of the target language, and they are not justified by the inter-changeability of the texts in the source language and the target language in one and the same position. The 'unbounded' translation is considered as 'free' translation, where equivalents shift freely up and down the rank scale. 'Word-for-word' translation is a 'rank-bound' translation. A 'literal' translation lies between the 'rank-bound' and 'free' translation. 'Literal' translation aims to be lexically 'word-for-word.'

'Phonological' translation is 'restricted' translation where the phonology of the source language text is substituted by equivalent phonology in the target language. The grammar and lexis of the source language text remain the same except the random grammatical or lexical deviations. In doing the phonological translation of the English plural cats to a language which has no final consonant clusters might be kat. The phonological translation equivalent ends it 't,' which seems to be a singular. The phonological translation equivalence is based on the relationship for the source language and the target language phonological units to the same phonic substance. As an example, Catford cites the phonological translation of had. He states, "the phonological translation of English 'had'/had/ into Greek is/xent/. The distinctive phonic substance related to English/h/is 'voiceless glottal fricative'—*i.e.*, a 'deep' voiceless fricative, that is, one in which the fricative hiss is generated by turbulent airflow through the flottis and modulated by the vocoid-shaping of the mouth. Greek has only one phoneme related to nearly the same phonic substance/x/—*i.e.*, a 'deep' voiceless fricative, the hiss here being generated by turbulent airflow through a channel formed between the dorsal surface of the tongue and the roof of the mouth and modulated by the vocoid-shaping of the mouth. The English/a/is a low front vocoid, and the same phonic features are present in Gk/e/ (although, in fact, the Gk, vowel is not so low as the English one—but each is the lowest in the front series of each language). English/d/is a voiced apical stop. Gk, has an apical stop/t/, but in Greek the components 'stop' and 'voice' co-occur only when a nasal precedes. The translation equivalent of English/d/therefore must either be Greek/t/, or Greek/nt/manifested phonetically as (nd): Greeks normally use the latter when speaking English with a 'Greek accent', *i.e.*, in phonological translation."[8]

Phonological translation, may change the rank or reorganize the aspects of substance into the target language's formal units. In normal total translation the phonology of the source language is not translated, but only replaced by whatever phonology of the target language is needed when selecting the grammatical and lexical items of the target language. In certain cases, however, the translator tries to reproduce some aspects of the phonology of the source language in the target language and this influences the grammatical and lexical translation, because the translation equivalents at these levels are selected partly by the requirement for their phonological exponents to be translation equivalents of phonological items in the source language. This occurs typically in case of film-dubbing. In translating poetry also, some trial may be made to select equivalents in the target language to match the sound of the items of the source language; this requires some degree of phonological translation.

'Graphological translation' is 'restricted translation' where the graphology of the source language text is substituted by equivalent graphology in the target language. The equivalence is based on the relationship to the same graphic substance. This translation is difficult, as the writing systems use a restricted range of graphic substance. An approximate graphological translation is done by typographers who want to give an 'exotic' flavour to written texts. For example, it can be seen that books about Islam or the Arab would sometimes have their titles written in Arabic-lie-script—a graphological semi-translation.

Transliteration is different from graphological translation. As Catford rightly says, "In transliteration, SL graphological units are replaced by TL graphological units; but these are not translation equivalents, since they are not selected on the basis of relationship to the same graphic substance."

In the process of actually transliterating a text, the transliterator replaces each SL letter or other graphological unit by a TL letter, or other unit, on the basis of a conventionally established set of rules. The transliteration rules specify transliteration-equivalents which differ from translation-equivalents in two ways: first, in not necessarily being relatable to the same graphic substance as the SL letters; secondly, in being (in good transliteration) in one-to-one correspondence with SL letters or other units.

In principle, the process of setting up a transliteration-system involves three steps:

(1) SL letters are replaced by SL phonological units; this is the normal literate process of converting from the written to the spoken medium.

(2) The SL phonological units are translated into TL phonological units.

(3) The TL phonological units are converted into TL letters, or other graphological units.[9]

The writing-system, where the letters or graphological units are in one-to-one correlation with phonological units or with parts of phonic substance, is considered as 'transcription.'

Phonological units are represented by this method, whereas graphological units are represented through 'transliteration.'

'Grammatical' translation is 'restricted' translation where the grammar of the source language text is substituted by equivalent grammar in the target language, but the lexis is not replaced. The equivalence is based on the relationship to the same situation-substance. 'Lexical' translation is 'restricted' translation where the lexis of a text is substituted by equivalent lexis in the target language, but the grammar is not changed. The equivalence is based on the relationship to the same situation-substance.

Some scholars made a distinction between vertical and horizontal translation. Medieval translation might be either vertical or horizontal. The translation into the native language from the source language (SL) which has a special value might be called vertical. But when both SL and TL have the same value, it is called horizontal translation. McGuire cites the case of Gianfranco Folena to make point clear:

> In his useful article on Vulgarization and translation, Gianfranco Folena suggests that medieval translation might be described either as vertical, by which he intends translation into the vernacular from a SL, that has special prestige or value (ex. Latin) or as horizontal, where both SL and TL have a similar value (ex. Provencal into Italian, Norman-French into English).[10]

The distinction between vertical and horizontal translation is useful because it shows how translation could be connected to two coexistent but distinct literary systems. While the vertical approach splits into two different types, the interlinear gloss, the horizontal translation includes imitation and borrowing.

In *Translating Poetry, Seven Strategies and a Blue Print* Andre Lefevere gives an interesting account of the various methods of translation in the following words:

(1) Phonemic translation, which attempts to reproduce the SL sound in the TL while at the same time producing an acceptable paraphrase of the sense. Lefevere comes to the conclusion that although this works moderately

well in the translation of onomatopoeia, the overall result is clumsy and often devoid of sense altogether.

(2) Literal translation, where the emphasis on word-for-word translation distorts the sense and the syntax of the original.

(3) Metrical translation, where the dominant criterion is the reproduction of the SL metre. Lefevere concludes that, like literal translation, this method concentrates on one aspect of the SL text at the expense of the text as a whole.

(4) Poetry into prose. Here Lefevere concludes that distortion of the sense, communicative value and syntax of the SL text results from this method, although not to the same extent as with the literal or metrical types of translation.

(5) Rhymed translation, where the translator 'enters into a double bondage' or metre and rhyme. Lefevere's conclusions here are particularly harsh, since he feels that the end product is merely a 'caricature' of Catullus.

(6) Blank *verse* translation. Again the restrictions imposed on the translator by the choice of structure are emphasized, although the greater accuracy and higher degree of literalness obtained are also noted.

(7) Interpretation. Under this heading, Lefevere discusses what he calls versions where the substance of the SL text is retained but the form is changed, and imitations where the translator produces a poem of his own which has 'only title and point of departure, if those, in common with the source text.' (qtd. in Bassnett-McGuire 81-82)

Another important writer Popvic distinguishes four types of translation in his discussion about translation equivalence. McGuire expresses the distinction made by Popvic in the following words:

(1) Linguistic equivalence, where there is homogeneity on the linguistic level of both SL and TL texts, *i.e.,* word-for-word translation.

(2) Paradigmatic equivalence, where there is equivalence of 'the elements of a paradigmatic expressive axis,' *i.e.*, elements of grammar, which Popvic sees as being a higher category than lexical equivalence.

(3) Stylistic (translational) equivalence, where there is 'functional equivalence of elements in both original and translation aiming at an expressive identity with an invariant of identical meaning.'

(4) Textual (syntagmatic) equivalence, where there is equivalence of the syntagmatic structuring of a text, *i.e.*, equivalence of form and shape.[11]

Interpreters take recourse to translation from SL into TL and *vice versa* in international meets of various kinds. Political leaders take the help of interpreters in communicating with foreign leaders. With the broadening of the base of the 'translation' its division into different types has acquired significance in our time.

## NOTES

1. Susan Bassnett-McGuire, quoted, *Translation Studies* (London: Routledge, 1991) 60.
2. G.E. Wellworth, "Special Consideration in Drama Translation," *Translation Spectrum: Essays in Theory and Practice* ed. M.G. Rose (New York: 1981) 143.
3. Chandrasekhar Patil, "Rhythm in Translation: Between the Words and Beyond Them," *Literature in Translation.* Ed. Pramod Talgeri and S.B. Verma (Bombay: Popular Prakashan, 1988) 170.
4. Maya Pandit, quoted, "The Problems of Translation," *The Literary Criterion* 22: 2 (1987): 57.
5. Roman Jakobson, "On Linguistic Aspects of Translation," *On Translation* ed. R.A. Brower (New York: Oxford University Press, 1966) 233.
6. J.C. Catford, *A Linguistic Theory of Translation* (London: Oxford University Press, 1965) 21.
7. *Ibid.*, 22.
8. *Ibid.*, 56.
9. *Ibid.*, 66.
10. McGuire, quoted, 52.
11. *Ibid.*, 25.

# 4

# Problems of Translation

Translation in the first place, is a transference of meaning from the Source Language to the Target Language. But what matters is not a translation of words from SL into TL, for exact equivalence of words of the former is hard to get in the latter. Translation is both linguistic and cultural activity and it is concerned with communication of meaning. It is not merely lexical equivalent of words of one language to that of another, (say, TL equivalent of SL words) but much more. Since each word is charged with memory, associations, and literary echoes, it is difficult to find full equivalence of an SL word in another word in TL. That is why, total or full translation is a myth.

What then, are the problems of translation? Ages ago Cicero summed up the translator's dilemma in the following words:

> If I render word for word, the result will sound uncouth and if compelled by necessity I alter anything in the order or wording, I shall seem to have departed from the function of a translator.[1]

A translator, in the first place, should possess an inwardness with both the languages—the source language (SL), from which the translation is to be made, and the target language (TL) into which the translation is to be done. He should have a mastery over both languages and the words should "obey his call." Above all, he should have the "feel" of the language. Secondly, in case of literature translation, literal translation should be avoided at all costs because it fails to carry the transposition of culture. The translator should not only give the lexical equivalent of words but keep in mind the socio-cultural matrix. Language is never a mechanical sound system, for each word is charged with memory, associations and literary allusions. Meenakshi Mukherjee makes an apt observation on this subject: (i) According to her, the act of translation is voluntary, that is the material has been chosen by the translator himself and the prime mover is a compelling desire to recreate. (ii) The translator is a writer in the language in which he is translating that is, his handling of the language is not merely competent but creative.[2] Since language is to some extent culture oriented, translators face the problem of translating certain culture-based words into another language with a different culture. For instance, Lord Krishna's "Rasa Krida" is difficult to translate into English. Similarly, the translation of "Love Play" for "Lila" seems to me inadequate and something is missing in such a translation. For example, a word like "abhimana" has no equivalent word in English and "Pique" is a poor translation of that great word which has a lot of associations in Indian context. Moreover, Indian languages (particularly, Sanskrit) are rich in erotic vocabulary, but English language with all its richness and luxury is very poor in erotic vocabulary. Thus, the transcreation of Vatsyayan's *Kamasutra* into English fails to carry the "feel" of original writing with it. Moreover, words like "uncle," "aunt," "brother-in-law," "cousin" have a lot of equivalent words in Indian languages. How can one translate these culture-based words and "swear words" without taking the context and the "whole" into consideration?

The translator has to make a balance between maintaining close fidelity to the original and utter freedom from it. Sri Aurobindo is in favour of taking liberty with the original. He states that "a translator is not necessarily bound to the original he chooses; he can make his own poem out of it, if he likes, and that is what is generally done."[3] Translation is neither "transliteration" nor "transcreation" and it has to guard against the danger of word for word literal translation as well as taking too much liberty. In the name of creation in the light of recent literary criticism which holds indeterminacy of meaning as its central concept, the art of translation has become increasingly difficult. If each word is a sign and each sign has a signifier and a signified and again a signified is also a signifier then which meaning should one take in translation? Should one take the signification (linguistic code) of a word or its value into consideration for translation?

The problems of translation are greatly enhanced by linguistic indeterminacy which is the result of perpetual change. Next to it is the uncertainty of knowing the meaning of the "text" accurately. In Literature translation the "text" is vital for it is the "text" that has to be rendered into another language. The indeterminacy of the text is a crucial concept in contemporary literary criticism. As Roland Barthes rightly observes "as a limiting case, an ideal text that is infinitely plural and contrasts it with the classical text (*i.e.*, text classique), which is characterized by a limited or parsimonious plurality of sense."[4] The author-text-reader triangle has undergone several changes in recent times. At one end stands the texts created by the author and at the other stands the reader who experiences it. The text controls the reader's response while the reader lends his own complexion to the text. Rajnath is right when he says that "out of the interaction between the text and the reader comes into existence the literary construct."[5] Wolfgang Iser maintains that any description of interaction between the two (the text and the reader) must therefore incorporate both the structure of effects (the text) and that of response (the reader).[6] Thus there are two "texts" now-one, the author's and another the reader's. Text is not what the author thought it to be but what the reader sees in it. Hence, the reader or the critic is the co-author and criticism is not an interpretation of the "text" but an extension of it. In such a state, what is the role of a translator and what will happen to translation? In addition to this there is the problem of the use of language in literature. If literary language is metaphorical, then which meaning should a translator take in translation, literal or metaphorical? "In a translation process," says A.K. Srivastava, "It is the metaphoric *metier* that provokes the problem of ambiguity even when assuming that the 'core' meaning arrived at by the translation represents the temper and tone of the original faithfully."[7]

What happens in translation? In the process a new category of 're-coding' takes place after 'de-coding' the SL text. Both linguistics and cultural factors shape the acts of 'de-coding' and 'en-coding.' The decoding of the message and meaning of the SL text into the encoding of message and meaning in the TL text, is what we understand by translation in our time. It is well neigh impossible to get an exact equivalent of the messages of the SL text in the target language. The indeterminacy of words and the elusive nature of language have made the task of the translator difficult. Even then the 'meaning' (*i.e.*, the overall meaning) of the SL text can be rendered into the target language. Let us turn to the translator who bears the burnt of translation.

The translator faces many problems while rendering a text from the source language into the target language. His task is more difficult than a creative writer for the latter thinks and writes in one language while the former has to make a tight-rope walking between two languages. In this chapter an attempt has been made to outline the problems faced by translations in general and the difficulties involved in the process of translation—particularly of jokes, humorous statements, poetry, drama and fiction. Culture and culture-words create a good deal of problems in translation.

Language is largely culture oriented and therefore, translators face the problem of translating certain culture based words into another language with a different culture. Colloquial expressions, culture-words, slangs, proverbs are difficult to translate for there is no one to one correspondence between one culture and another or one language and another. Equivalence of words in two or more languages is hard to come by. Hence, the difficulty arises in finding equivalent swear words in another language. Socio-cultural matrix plays a vital role in checking the nuances of the words in both languages—SL and TL. Here are a few culture-words that pose a good deal, problem in translation: 'Abhiman' (Pique), Krishna 'Lila,' 'Dharma,' 'Rasakrida' (love-play) and a host of others (mentioned earlier) make the life of the translator miserable.

The influence of LI (language one, *i.e.*, mother-tongue) on the use of English by Indian readers creates sentences like 'I am feeling cold' instead of 'I feel cold,' 'I am loving her' instead of 'I love her,' 'I am liking you' instead of 'I like you', etc. which are un-English in feature. 'To translate is to change into another language, retaining as much of the sense as one can,'[8] says A.H. Smith. But retaining the sense alone is not enough. We have to maintain the semantic compatibility along with grammaticality.

Let's take the question of literal translation. R.S. Pathak gives an interesting account of such a type of translation in the following words:

> Literal translation has its advantages and limitations which need to be weighed carefully for each cultural element and lexical item. If we translate screwdriver as 'penchkus' for example, it is fully acceptable. But what about I'm all eyes? 'Block' in American English means 'a rectangular section of a city or town bounded on each side by consecutive streets' or 'a segment of a street bounded by successive cross streets.' I do not think there is any exact equivalent for block in Hindi which can be helpful in translating a sentence like "We used to live on the same block." Words like sacred, secular, communal convey different shades of meaning to different people. Different races have different notions of 'incest' and therefore, the word will have no uniform meaning for them. The term gentleman cannot be rendered faithfully in Hindi; even 'sambhrant,' borrowed from Sanskrit, does not really serve the purpose nor does the Bengali 'bhadralog.' The problem becomes all the more obvious in technical and semi-technical writings. It is not correct to translate, for example, terms like 'pradakshina path,' 'vedika' and 'toran' as 'circumambulatory path,' 'railing' and 'gateways' respectively, as has been done in a very recent edition of *The Hindustan Times,* for the real sense of the original terms evaporates as soon as they are given in English as above. Terms from Indian Poetics like 'rasa,' 'vakrokti' are just untranslatable into English. This is also true of scores of words from the spheres of philosophy, grammar and Indian system of medicine.

Nothing would be gained if pig iron and silver fish are rendered in Hindi as 'sookarayask' and 'rajat matsya' respectively.

A word-forward translation of the phrase heat and cold will be 'garmi aur sardi' or 'sardi garmi.' A Herculean task, in all propriety, should be rendered as 'Bhagirath Prayatna' rather than 'Herculeus ka Karya.' Translating stadium as 'Prashal' shows inventiveness, but such cases are rare. Raghuvir circulated quite a few expressions which have failed to find any acceptance. Some of these words are: 'kanthlangote' (necktie), 'dhumraddhavaldandika' (cigarette), 'louhpathgamini' (train) and so on. 'Preshmudrank' for postal stamp, and 'Netrak' for spectacles also belong to the same category. A common expression too too mein mein 'communicate far too much than its translated version you youing me meing suggested by P. Lal and N. Napony. A literal translation of some typical expressions would be ridiculous."[9]

Homonymns of Indian languages (*i.e.*, the same form in several Indian languages) create problems for the translators. For example 'damn' in Bengali means 'big' but it is used as an objective to Oriya words 'darun dukh' ('great sorrow') or 'darun aghat' ('great shock'). I am inclined to quote R.S. Pathak again who gives a whole list of such homonymns in the following passage:

> The problem gets compounded because the same form gives different meanings in different languages. For example 'uphar' in Marathi signifies 'refreshment,' but it means in Hindi 'a present,' and 'uttejit' means 'inspired' in Marathi and 'angry or a agitated' in Hindi, 'Shiksha' in Hindi is 'teaching or education' and in Marathi 'punishment,' 'Razinama' is used in Marathi in the sense of 'resignation,' but in Hindi it means 'agreement.' Similarly, the word 'ashuddh' means in Hindi 'incorrect' or 'impure'; in Kashmiri it means 'very precious' (thing) and also 'medicine' or 'cure.' 'Jal' in Hindi is 'water' but 'zal' in Kashmiri is 'urine.' 'Manhoos' in Kashmiri means 'unsocial, shy, gloomy' and in Hindi 'ominous' or 'inauspicious.' Such 'false friends' and deceptive cognates will only make the translator's task further complicated. Polysemy and oligosemy, like lexical gaps, also obstruct successful translatability. Moreover, the translator should be able to differentiate between the

denotative, connotative and idiomatic meanings of words. Then, words come to acquire certain associations in languages. According to Bertrand Russell, "no one can understand the word 'cheese' unless he has a non-linguistic acquaintance with cheese."[10] Some words gain in due course semitonic function like nodding or shaking of the head or pointing. Roman Jakobson rightly points out that "we distinguish three ways of interpreting a verbal sign; it may be translated into other signs of the same language, into another language, or into another non-verbal system of symbols." Because of their undertones of connotative meanings translation of some words becomes still more problematic. A couple of examples will make it clear. Dove in Bengali is not a symbol of peace; it is equivalent of a cunning, unprincipled person who drives people out of their homes. The word 'dushta' in Bengali is the highest abuse and conveys far more than what it does in Hindi and other cognate languages. 'Reja' has two meanings in Orissa alone; in and around Sambalpur it means a 'woman worker,' but in other dialects of Oriya it stands for 'change or loose coins' (*Critical Practice* 100-101).

Certain food items of India and words of common use in everyday conversation based on culture cannot be translated accurately into a foreign tongue. For example

> 'the Indian' delicacies like halva, puri, kheer, jalevi thus cannot be sensibly translated into (Italian) spaghetti, maccheroni, minestrone and pizzas. The English soft drinks means something different in our country. In Serbo-Croatian it is bezalkoholna piea, literally 'without-alcohol drinks.' In West African English, however, we have not drinks, 'alcoholic drinks.' Other culture-bound expressions from the same language are: "chewing stick (twig used for cleaning teeth), cover shoulder (a blouse), knocking fee (money paid by a man to a woman's family for initiating negotiations about marriage), outdooring (the first appearance of a baby in public), sleeping cloth (cloth on which one sleeps at night), small room (toilet) and tight friend (close friend),"[11] rightly says R.S. Pathak (*CP* 101).

Thus literal translation and translation based on culture words are beset with pitfalls.

Cultural words create problems, as the impact of them gets lost in the process of translation. For example, the simple word 'you' in English has three corresponding words in most of the Indian languages including Oriya. In Oriya it means 'Tu,' 'Tame' and 'Apana'. depending upon the relationship with the person to whom the speaker addresses. English words like 'cousin,' 'uncle,' 'aunt' have a number of corresponding words in Indian languages and therefore, translation of these words into Indian languages becomes ambiguous. Take for instance a sentence like, "My uncle came yesterday" which when rendered into Oriya may mean either my father's brother or brother-in-law or my mother's brother or brother-in-law came (even, an explanation like paternal uncle or maternal uncle will not do). In Oriya we have a term 'Samudi' that explains the relationship between two persons whose son and daughter get married and become husband and wife respectively. In English we have no equivalent words for these Oriya words 'Samudi' or for that mater his wife 'Samuduni.' How to translate these words? That's a Herculean task.

English is SVO (subject, verb, object) language but most of the Indian languages including Oriya are SOV (subject, object, verb) languages. And moreover when we use simple present tense in English, in Indian languages we use present progressive tense. Take for example the Oriya sentences like "Mun Sabu Januchi" (I am knowing everything), 'Sabu Sunuchi' (am hearing) 'bujhuchi' (am understanding) produce ungrammaticalities if translated 'word for word' into English. The Oriya users of English is confused by tense and aspect. "I have seen him last week" is incorrect in English but if translated word for word into Oriya becomes correct grammatically.

The translation of literature poses a good deal of problems for the translator. Literature translation involves not only the transference of meaning but a host of associations charged with the meaning which need to be translated from SL text into TL text. Since the basic loss of meaning is one a continuum between under translation and over translation, it is imperative on our part to divide literature translation genrewise. First, I take up the problems of poetry translation.

Once Robert Frost said, 'Poetry is that which is lost in translation.' If a good deal of poetry is lost, enough is retained in translation. No doubt, poetry translation poses formidable challenge to the translator. The most difficult thing in poetry translation is to find equivalent words of literary echoes in target language. For example, how to find out equivalent words of Eliot's use of Spenser's line 'Sweet Thames...?' And again the barrier to meaning is not simply cultural, even those sharing the same language may not get the allusions correctly. Does the English-knowing readers recognise Eliot's allusion to 'Prothalamion' in *The Wasteland*?

Secondly, the problem of language in poetry is not easy to overcome. Ornamental words (rhetoric) based on lyricism are almost impossible to translate. I am inclined to agree with Jayanta Mahapatra, the well-known Indian English poet and translator when he draws our attention to the difficulty of Poetry translation in the following words:

> It is generally believed that a verse translation is itself poetry, but whether it really is poetry or not is a questionable matter. Any poem will not move fluently into translation, my own experience reveals the many hazards and difficulties encountered in the process. My main concern being from Oriya into English, I shall discuss some of these. For example, it is almost impossible to translate poets like Upendra Bhanja or Gangadhar Mehere. In Oriya literature the problem is of language, basically—and this fact is especially noticeable with these earlier poets, poets who used language with such powers of magic and devotion that resulted in instilling in readers' minds a divine and perhaps mystic presence. Neither Upendra Bhanja nor Gangadhar Mehere used free verse, and their poems literally sag with the weight of ornamentation and alliterative sounds. Lyrical poetry such as they wrote was full of words having too many referential allusions, and was more or less ritualistic, with an incantatory tone. For that matter, I would feel uncomfortable when I heard such

> a poem being recited aloud, as though I were undergoing a mystic sort of experience. Even the later poets of the Oriya language, like Radhanath Ray, resorted to strict, musical verse forms—something that fed the poetry with a feeling of mysteriousness. Oriya diction is slow and formal, the sounds of words seem to dig into the mind and meander in the deeper layers of the imagination. Let us consider the first four lines of the poem "Chilika" by Radhanath Ray:
>
> Utkata-kamala bilasa-dirghika
> Marala malini nilambu Chilika
> Utkalara thui charu alankara
> Utkala bhubane shobhara bhandara
>
> How very clever, how concise is the construction of this verse form! And with what perfection has the poet woven the sounds of each line! How very much does each line convey, with its sensual, archaic flavour! Into the four words of each line is compressed the deep passion of the poet; and how does one translate a compact verse form of this type into a foreign medium such as English? To me, a good translation into English seems almost impossible to make. For the verse resembles a many-petalled flower, each petal having its own word-significance, its individual auditory echoes. To render gems like these into English would be futile exercise, which would only harm the poetry in the original Oriya, like an act of desecration one can't pardon.[12]

In a poem sounds, rhythm, words, images, symbols, etc. are not only present together, but they also act on one another. That is why, reading poetry is itself an act of creative interpretation. Rendering a poem into another language, becomes an act of 'creative transposition,' as Jakobson would make us believe. The translator is a guide and a reader and therefore his act of reading (perusal) becomes co-terminus with his reading (meaning) of it. What Hugh Kenner says is that "As the poet begins by seeing, so the translator by reading; but his reading must be a kind of seeing."[13]

The greatest problem when translating a text (*i.e.*, a poem) from a distant past is not that 'the poet and his contemporaries are dead but the significance of the poem in its context is dead,'[14] says McGuire and rightly so. It is often argued that translation is not interpretation. The job of the translator is to reproduce what the author says not what he means. McGuire refutes such a claim with illustration in the following way:

> It has often been argued, in accordance with Longfellow, that translation and interpretation are two separate activities, and that it is the duty of the translator to translate what is there and not to 'interpret' it. The fallacy of such an argument is obvious—since every reading is an interpretation, the activities cannot be separated. James Holmes has devised the following useful diagram to show the interrelationship between translation and critical interpretation.

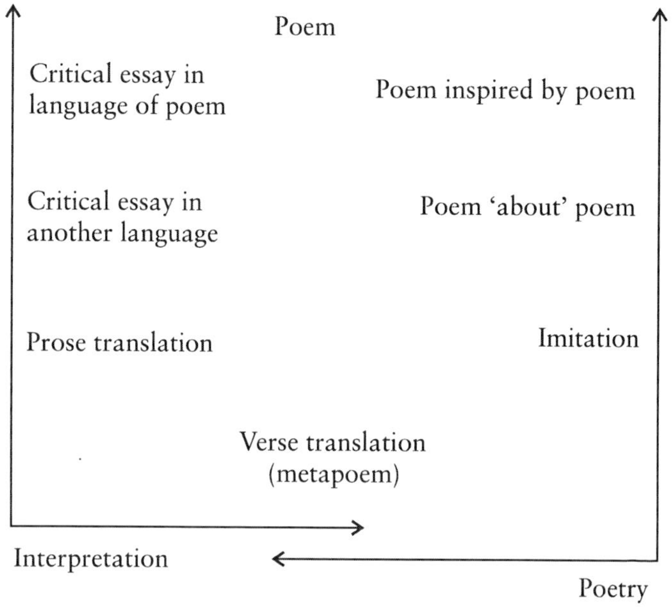


The verse translation rests on the axis point where types of interpretation intersect with types of imitation and derivation. Moreover, a translator will continue to produce 'new' versions of a given text, not so much to reach an ideal 'percent translation' but because each previous version, being context bound, represents a reading accessible to the time in which it is produced, and moreover is individualistic. William Morris' versions of Homer or of Beowulf are both idiosyncratic in that they spring from Morris' own system of priorities and commitment to archaic form and language, and they are Victorian in that they exemplify a set of canons distinctive to one period in time. The great difference between a text and a meta text is that the one is fixed in time and place, and other is variable. There is only one Divina Commedia but there are innumerable readings and in theory innumerable translations.[15]

Great poetry taps the mythic reserves of human experience and it also creates myths which provide a meta-language for the social and cultural meanings. The new meanings a work of art creates, are foregrounded in the traditional meanings and therefore, in a work of art there is always a tension between the two sets of meanings. That adds to the problems of the translator. Take for instance, Keats' "Ode to a Nightingale." The poem is imbued with cultural meanings. Keats' idea of nightingale has something to do with the western core and somehow it becomes a universal symbol. As K. Chellappan has rightly pointed out that "this basic symbol is evolved in relation to other symbols in the poem, which again are generated in the context of the poem, though they also have traditional links. If the ultimate meaning of the poem depends on all these facts, and if some of the components like Ruth or Hippocrene belong to the particular milieu, what do we do with them? Equivalents in the target culture may not do, because they bring a whole world of associations."[16]

Translation of poetry is the most difficult mode of translation. This is because it abounds in figures of speech such as similes, metaphors, irony, paradox, etc. and unprecedented phonological, syntactic and semantic patterns such as rhyming alliteration, versification, morphological parallelism, syntactic parallelism and above all syntagmatic and paradigmatic relations between words. The translator of poetry should remember that he is to 'translate' a piece of poetry, not to 're-write' or 'produce an interpretation' of it.

The translator of poetry must take into account both the linguistic and non-linguistic aspects of a poem and try to re-create the poem in the target language. The linguistic aspect deals with sound pattern of words, rhymes and rhythms while the non-linguistic aspect is concerned with ideas, images, symbols based on culture of the SL poem. Some translators plead for prose rendering of a poem while others argue in favour of 'verse for verse' translation. This brings to our mind the difference between the poetry of earlier ages which was written in metre and rhyme, and the modern poetry in free-verse. It is easier to translate prose-poems (or poems written in free verse) into another language. But traditional poetry with its rhyme, metre and sound poses great problem for the translators. The translator should have the 'feel' of the poem; otherwise it will not be possible to translate it into TL. It should be borne in mind that even when adequate translation of poetry is not possible, there is no need for the translator to raise his hand in despair and say that poetry is not translatable. In spite of all the difficulties, translation of poetry is done for the benefit of the readers in the target language. Changing Robert Frost's dictum, we will say that poetry is that which is survived in translation. Translation of dramatic texts pose another kind of problem. Dialogues in dialects of a language that is far removed from the target language are very difficult to translate. Apart from language, the thought-content of a dramatic text couched in one culture poses serious problems for the translator. For example, it is difficult to translate Shakespeare and his contemporaries into any Indian language because of the linguistic and cultural differences. For example, how does one translate the magical words of Shakespeare, 'Ripeness is all,' or 'Forget and Forgive' or 'Thou art soul in bliss, I'm bound upon wheel of Fire' or 'Fair is Foul and Foul is Fair' or 'The rest is silence', etc. into our languages which are so vastly different from English language?

Furthermore, a dramatic text exhibits its full meaning only in its performance. As Anne Ubersfeld says that "The task of the director, therefore, is to 'translate into another language' a text of which he has a prime duty to remain 'faithful.' This position is based on the concept of semantic equivalence between the written text and its performance, only the 'mode of expression' in Hjelmslevian sense of the term will be altered, the form and content of the expression will remain identical when transferred from a system of test-signs to a system of performance-signs."[17]

The problem of performability is further complicated by the changing concepts of performance. Let us take the case of Shakespearean dramatic texts. In his time young boys were acting as heroines and Shakespeare introduced the technique of disguise according to which the heroine went in search of the hero into the forest. Nowadays can a director think of such a technique in theatre? On the other hand, modern Absurd dramatists and dramatists of Angry Young Man Movement pose another kind of problem for the translator. The dialogues, and performance create special problems for the translator and the director. How does one translate the dialogues of Lucky and Pozzo or Estragon and Vladimir of Beckett's *Waiting for Godot* into Indian languages?

Thus, the dialogues, performance, including stage-craft create problems for the translator. The colloquial and conversational language, intonation and accent including dialogue-delivery make the translation of dramatic texts difficult.

The translation of prose texts including novels pose another kind of problem. Hilaire Belloc outlined six general rules for the translator of prose texts:

(1) The translator should not 'plod on,' word by word or sentence by sentence, but should 'always "block out" his work.' By 'block out,' Belloc means that the translator should consider the work as an integral unit and translate in sections, asking himself 'before each what the whole sense is he has to render.'

(2) The translator should render idiom by idiom 'and idioms of their nature demand translation into another form from that of the original.' Belloc cites the case of the Greek exclamation 'By the Dog!,' which, if rendered literally, becomes merely coming in English, and suggests that the phrase 'By God!' is a much closer translation. Likewise, he points out that the French historic present must be translated into the English narrative tense,

which is past, and the French system of defining a proposition by putting it into the form of a rhetorical question cannot be transposed into English where the same system does not apply.

(3) The translator must render 'intention by intention,' bearing in mind that 'the intention of a phrase in one language may be less emphatic than the form of the phrase, or it may be more emphatic.' By 'intention,' Belloc seems to be talking about the weight a given expression may have in a particular context in the SL that would be disproportionate if translated literally into the TL. He quotes several examples where the weighting of the phrase in the SL is clearly much stronger or much weaker than the literal TL translation, and points out that in the translation of 'intention,' it is often necessary to add words not in the original 'to conform to the idiom of one's own tongue.'

(4) Belloc warns against *les faux* aims, those words or structures that may appear to correspond in both SL and TL but actually do not, *e.g.*, demander—to ask, translated wrongly as to demand.

(5) The translator is advised to 'transmute boldly' and Belloc suggests that the essence of translating is 'the resurrection of an alien thing in a native body.'

(6) The translator should never embellish.[18]

Belloc's points are significant for they emphasize both themes and techniques. He attributes moral responsibility to the translator but at the same time gives him the liberty to change the text to suit the needs of the TL text reader. McGuire makes a pertinent comment on this point:

> Belloc's first point, in which he discusses the need for the translator problem for the prose translator: the difficulty of determining translation units. It must be clear at the outset that the text, understood to be in a dialectical relationship with other texts and located within a specific historical context, is the prime unit. But whereas the poet translator can more easily break the prime text down into translatable

units, *e.g.*, lines, verses, stanzas, the prose translator has a more complex task. Certainly, many novels are broken down into chapters or sections, but as Barthes has shown with his methodology of five reading codes (see S/Z, discussed by T. Hawkes, Structuralism and Semiotics, London, 1977) the structuring of a prose text is by no means as linear as the chapter divisions might indicate. Yet if the translator takes each sentence or paragraph as a minimum unit and translates it without relating it to the overall work, he runs the risk of ending up with a TL text like those quoted above, where the paraphrasable content of the passages has been translated at the cost of everything else.

The way round this dilemma must once again be sought through considering the function both of the text and of the devices within the text itself. If the translators of Silone had considered the function of the tone they would have understood why the careful rhetorical patterning of the opening paragraph needed closer examination. Likewise, if the translator of Mann had considered the function of the description of both the young man and the journey, she would have understood the reasons for Mann's choice of language. Every prime text is made up of a series of interlocking systems, each of which has a determinable function in relation to the whole, and it is the task of the translator to apprehend these functions.[19]

Having outlined the problems of different types of literary texts, I should turn to the problems of translating jokes and problems of specialized translations. It is said that humour is universal but joke is local. Unless one knows the exact nature or origin of the joke it would not be possible for one to translate it into another language. A research on jokes based on group studies conducted by M. Radhika and Udayanarayan Singh classifies jokes into the following 13 types:

(1) Ethnic jokes include jokes on people who are stingy, unclean, dumb, or about those who show blind obedience, language distortion, or are cunning, etc. These are usually associated with a particular sect or a group.

(2) Political jokes expose political situations, state pressions, national traits, defamation of political figures, etc. Since politics affects the whole nation, these are usually immensely popular jokes.

(3) Sexual jokes include jokes on adultery, obscenity, sexual ignorance, sexual prowess, etc.

(4) Religious jokes cover jokes that deal with religious subjects including priests, nuns and Gods as the butts.

(5) Economy jokes relate to shortage, poverty, etc. of a particular group of community or nation. Since any kind of deviance can provide one with a potential source of humour, economic deprivation cannot be avoided.

(6) Stupid or Aging jokes cover jokes on aging, idiocy, irrationality, etc.

(7) Clever repartees are actually witty, wacky and deliberate insults. One instance should suffice: John (handling a chocolate): Here, honey, sweets to the sweet. Mary: Oh, Thank you. Won't you have some of these nuts.

(8) Anti-Social jokes are jokes on drinking, stealing, terrorism, etc.

(9) Uniform jokes are about the military, flying and sailing crews, waiters, police, etc.

(10) Academic jokes relate to all academic institutions, and especially to student-student and student-teacher interactions.

(11) Professional jokes cover all professions such as lawyers, doctors, businessmen, bureaucrats, clerks, and others.

(12) Family jokes deal with all members of a family—grand-parents, parents and children, grand-children or other relatives.

(13) Linguistic jokes, *i.e.*, spoonerisms, misprints, ghostwriting, daffy definition, puns, parodies, mistakes, etc. may come under this category.[20]

The problematic jokes are very difficult to translate. They are based on homonymy, polysemy and with double meaning due to literal and figurative interpretations. There are no definite rules or established norms to interpret and translate texts—much less to evaluate it.

Research shows that all jokes are translatable. But he does not try for a Sabun saree. The following observations are made to find out how humour can grip a human mind:

(1) All jokes are translatable. But the translation of only some kind of jokes produce humorous effect similar to the one produced by the SL joke.

(2) The method of translation adopted was neither very free or very faithful. The translators aiming for dynamic equivalence.

(3) No two translations of the same joke were alike.

(4) The devices adopted for the translation of the body of jokes is similar to that of non-humorous tests. The punch line is to be translated in such a way that humour is retained as in the source text.

(5) When metaphors or idioms were present in the body of text, the sence was translated.

(6) Jokes based on double meanings due to literal and figurative meanings, polysemy, homonymy and misprints were problematic. The translation of such types of jokes were attempted by adopting the devices of transcription and paraphrasing.

(7) The type of audience and the context within a joke is to be told or situated are both very important for translating jokes.

(8) The evaluations of SL jokes on the basis of 'funniness' and the evaluations of their translations on the basis of their translation techniques were similar, which shows that the translations were evaluated on the basis of the humorous content in the SL joke. In other words, the degree of funniness of the SL joke coloured the evaluation of the translation in TL. This fact was further corroborated when the TL (Telugu) texts were circulated around to elicit reaction/evaluation of these jokes

> (without showing them as translation) as if they were the originals. The results in both cases only confirmed the hypothesis that evaluation of retelling of jokes (in an other tongue) depends on the fun or humour they generate or retain rather than on the faithfulness to the SL text or such other measurement criterion.[21]

The problems of translation are many-fold but two major problems that baffle the translators are linguistic and cultural. Again, of all types of translation, the most elusive one is that of the translation of poetry. Two of our distinguished scholar-critics Sri Aurobindo and K.R.S. Iyengar have cautioned us while translating poetry into a second language. Iyengar says:

> Poetry by its very nature is untranslatable Ideas can be translated from language to language, but poetry is the idea touched with the magic of phrase and incantatory music. Competent translator can, however, play the good broker between the poet and the reader, and surpassing the mere prose of statement can give intimations of the poet's sovereign utterance. Good translation can create trust and it can stimulate interest.[22]

Sri Aurobindo is of the opinion that there are two ways of translating poetry: "One to keep it strictly to the manner and turn of the original, (and) the other is to take its spirit, sense and imagery and produce them freely so as to suit the new language." To Aurobindo the second method of translating poetry is preferable. But this is a more difficult path, as is evident from the following admission from Krishna Srinivas, himself an able translator.[23] He preferred the second method to the first.

T.S. Eliot on the other hand takes Gilbert Murray to task for the English translation of Medeka and complains about the translator's stretching "the Greek brevity to fit the loose frame of William Morris" and blurring "the Greek lyric to the fluid haze of Swinburne."[24] And Matthew Arnold found fault with all the three translators of Homer's *Illiad*. He wrote in "On Translating Homer":

> Homer is rapid in his movement, Homer is plain in his words and style, Homer is simple in his ideas. Homer is

> noble in his manner. Cowper renders him ill because he is slow in his movement, and elaborate in his style; Pope renders him ill because he is fantastic in his ideas; Mr. Newman renders him ill because he is odd in his words and ignoble in his manner.[25]

Translation of metaphors pose a special kind of problem and the translator's burden is how to translate metaphors without affecting the SL discourse. Cultural factors cause difficulties in the translation of metaphors. For instance 'owl' in Oriya symbolizes 'ill fortune' whereas it is the symbol of wisdom in English, 'Bull' is the symbol of endurance in English whereas it is the symbol of rudeness in Persian.

In spite of all the problems that threaten the authenticity of translation and undermine its position, the desire to translate on the part of scholars and translators has shown an upward trend. Translation in the midst of all the problems, continues to be rendered, is something one should rejoice Ironically enough, it is the problems that make the art of translation challenging and finally fascinating.

## NOTES

1. Susan Bassnett-McGuire, quoted, *Translation Studies* (New York: Routledge, 1991) 43.
2. Meenakshi Mukherjee, "Transposition of Culture," *Cygnus* 2: 2 (1981): 73-74.
3. Premananda Kumar, "Translation: A Creative Process," *Cygnus* 2: 2 (1981): 65.
4. Roland Barthes, "Sign, Sense and Roland," *Literary Criticism Idea and Act* (Barkeley: University of California Press, 1974) 235.
5. Rajnath, "The Text and the Reader: Critique of Reader Response Criticism," *Journal of Literary Criticism* 3: 1 (1986): 19.
6. Wolfgang Iser, *The Act of Reading* (Baltimore: John Hopkin University Press, 1980) 21.
7. A.K. Srivastava, "On Translating Literature," *The Literary Criterion* 22: 2 (1987): 19.
8. A.H. Smith, ed., *Aspects of Translation* (London: Seeker and Warburg, 1958) VII.
9. R.S. Pathak, "Untranslatability: Myth or Reality," *Critical Practice* 2: 1 (June 1994): 99-100.

10. Bertrand Russell, "Logical Positivism," *Revue Internationale de Philosophie* 4 (1950): 18.
11. Pathak 100-01.
12. Jayanta Mahapatra, "Translating from the Oriya: An Approach," *Cygnus* 2: 2 (1981): 27-28.
13. Hugh Kenner, 'Introduction,' *The Translations of Ezra Pound* (London: Faber and Faber, 1953) 10.
14. McGuire 83.
15. *Ibid.*, 100-01.
16. K. Chellappan, "The Paradox of Transcreation," *Literature in Translation* ed. Pramod Talgeri and S.B. Verma (Bombay: Popular Prakashan, 1988) 167.
17. McGuire (Quoted) 121.
18. Hilaire Belloc, *On Translation* (Oxford: The Clarendon Press, 1931).
19. McGuire 117-18.
20. M. Radhika and Udayanarayan Singh, "Translation of jokes: Problems of Specialized Translation," *Critical Practice* 1: 2 (1994): 63.
21. *Ibid.*, 91-92.
22. Krishna Srinivas (Quoted), "On Translating Poetry," *Creative Forum* 1: 1 (1988): 52.
23. Sri Aurobindo, *The Future Poetry* (Pondicherry: Sri Aurobindo Birth Centenary Publication) 432.
24. T.S. Eliot, *The Sacred Wood* (London: Methuen, 1920) 71-77.
25. Matthew Arnold, *Essays, Literary and Critical* (London, 1950) 250.

# 5

# Translation as Creative Writing

Scholars and translators have viewed translation as new writing and a creative process disregarding the traditional notion that it is a mere rendering of SL text into TL text. It has rightly been observed that the best translation is one which does not read like translation at all. That is, perhaps the paradox of translation. It is replete with the excitement and joy of a voyage of discovery normally associated with an original work. In the light of recent critical theories, the concept of language and writing *vis-à-vis* literature has undergone a sea change. If it is the language that speaks not man ('language speaks, not man'—Heidegger) and Terence Hawkes' assertion 'Writing Writes, not authors'[1] then how does one envisage the role of a translator and the art of translation? As a critic deconstructs (decentres) the text and then reconstructs (recentres) it, so a translator de-codes an SL text and then re-codes it in the target language. If criticism has become creative, for it not only interprets the text but extends the meaning of it, then translation is creative for it re-creates an SL text in a new way in the target-language. The attempt in this chapter will be to show why translation should be taken as creative writing (or new writing).

Translator is a reader, an interpreter and a creator—all in one. In ancient India translation was regarded as a new writing. Sri Aurobindo is quoted to have said that "a translator is not necessarily bound to the original he chooses: he can make his own poem out of it, if he likes, and that is what is generally done."[2]

Prema Nandakumar reminds us of the ancient Indian literary tradition and implicity suggests that translation in this country was always given the status of new writing. She writes:

> The roots of India's *sanatana dharma* are to be found in the Vedas, the Upanishads and the Itihasas (the *Ramayana* and the *Mahabharata)*, all of which were originally indicated in Sanskrit. Through these many centuries enterprising translators have acted as life-giving rays of the Sun to produce this unparalleled Indian literature of today, truly an immense banyan tree with its luscious foliage of many languages.[3]

Our literary tradition of writing commentaries on the *Upanishads,* the *Gita* or the translation of stories from the *Ramayana* and the *Mahabharata* enables us to take translation as new writing. Old classics in our country have undergone translations into several regional languages and in each case the translation has been regarded as new writing. For example, the *Ramayana* and the *Mahabharata* have been rendered into a number of regional languages of India and all these renderings have been considered as 'new writings' (or creative writings) rather than imitations. So, we have Sarala Das' *The Mahabharata* in Oriya, Kasiram Das' version in Bengali, Viswanath Satyanarayan's in *Ramayana Kalpa Vrukshamu* in Telugu and in our century C. Rajgopalachari's translations into English of both the epics, *The Ramayana* and *The Mahabharata* have been considered not only popular but also examples of 'New Writing' (or creative writing).

K. Ayyappa Paniker gives an interesting account of the evolution of translation and its status in our country in the following lines:

> Talking about Indian perspectives on the translation of literature, it may be said that till the 19th century Indian 'translators' were not affected unduly by this anxiety of being true to the original in letter and spirit. All through the Middle Ages, throughout the length and breadth of India, Sanskrit classics like the epics and puranas continued to be retold, adapted, subverted, and "translated" without worrying about the exactness and accuracy of formal equivalence. When Kamban wrote *Ramayanam* in Tamil, he took all the freedom he needed to make his version of Valmiki's *Ramayana*, a Tamil classic. He keeps close to the

structure of Dravidian epic; he edits, cuts, condenses, elaborates, interprets, modifies, etc. to suit his own tastes as well as those of his immediate readers. The features of the target language and the tastes of the target readers at the time of translation are among the factors that promoted this free style translation. The 12th century Malayalam version *Ramacharitam*, like Tulasidasa's *Ramacharitamanas* or *Kritivas Ramayana*, is almost a new creation with shift of emphasis and occasionally substantial modification of episodes. Even *Adhyaatmaramayana* in Sanskrit is different in significant ways from Valmikiramayana. There are many versions of folk Ramayana like the Malayalam work *Sitadukham* which is almost a "feminist" version of the patriarchal text favoured by the elite. The impression one gets from all these multiple versions is that, not only was literal adherence to the original not insisted on, but that deviation was liberally tolerated, even encouraged and preferred. Even in the medieval Malayalam renderings of texts like *Bhagavadgita*, *Arthasastra* and *Brahmanda Purana*, this creative freedom was cherished and maintained. There is scope here for propounding the theory of translation as appropriation through linguistic manipulation. The Aryan or Sanskrit texts were localized in the South, even Dravidianized. The Bhakti Movement which gained momentum with the works of the Alwars and the spread of Bhagavatam was a process of desanskritization rather than of sanskritization. The non-Vedic Gods entered the pantheon and old rituals, even tribal customs, were accepted and absorbed. Some of the textual variants in the medieval translation seem to illustrate this. The politics of medieval Indian translations could perhaps be understood and interpreted in terms of the visible absence of the anxiety of authenticity on the part of these "translators." If the local/regional versions of *Ramayana* and *Mahabharata* became the classics of the regional literatures, the reason is not far to seek. These adapted translations were well received by the public in each region. There was nothing "alien" about them.[4]

The translations of classics into regional languages were taken as 'new writings' or 'creative writings.' Indian literary tradition takes translation as an autonomous creation equal to that of creative writing. Two significant anthologies of translation of our time, namely *New Writing in India* (1974) edited by Adil Jussawalla, and *Another India* (1990) edited jointly by Nissim Ezekiel and Meenakshi Mukherjee bear testimony to how translations read like New Writings. In our country we have numerous examples of translation being regarded as 'New Writing' (*i.e.,* Creative Writing). A translation theorist, Sujit Mukherjee who has done research in this field observes:

> New literary texts derived from *itihasa* or *purana* are obvious examples of this process. The erratic passage of Gunadhya's *Brihatakatha* into other languages would be a more typical instance of how later authors used an existing story and remade it to suit their own purposes. Similarly, when the Bengali poet Alaol produced a 17th century Bangla version of Malik Muhammad Jayasi's work in 15th century Avadhi, *Padumavat,* he provided a good illustration of a text from one modern Indo-Aryan language being re-told with modifications in another modern Indo-Aryan language. More often, of course, the original text would be in Sanskrit, and even minor work like the first one telling the tragic story of the musician Madhavanala and the dancer Kamakandala could get involved in his process. Apart from various Sanskrit versions, it is also available in Gujarati, Marathi, and Hindi—in the latter language alone there are at least six versions. The Hindi version by Alam, poet in Aurangzib's Court, is apparently based on a Sanskrit version by Jodh, a poet in Akbar's Court, and Jodh based his poem on Madhavanalakatha, a Sanskrit work in campus form composed in the 10th century or earlier, by Anandadhara. Alam admits in his opening verses that apart from what he had himself composed, he has translated from a Sanskrit poem and also borrowed from the Hindi versions of other poets.[5]

The concept of translation as creative writing can be better understood if we examine the job of self-translators and transcreators. Self-translators and bilingual writers take liberty with the original writing and write in a different way in the target language. Tagore's *Gitanjali* in English is vastly different from the original Bengali version of the poem. Manoj Das a bilingual fiction writer in Oriya and English wrote me to say that he does not translate literally from one language into another. For example, if he writes a short story first in Oriya, then he allows sometime to pass before writing it in English. Keeping the plot intact, he takes liberty with the details and transcreates it in English. So his stories are not translations into the target language but new writings. The same is the case with many bilingual writers of our country. These writers write in their mother-tongue (*i.e.*, Language 1) and also in the second language (language two or second language, that is usually, English). Their writings in both L1 and L2 should be taken as 'new writings' or creative writings—not translations from SL into TL.

Transcreation (P. Lal's term) means recreating an SL text in the target language taking absolute liberty with it and yet being fidel to it. The renderings of *The Ramayana* and *The Mahabharata* into English by R.K. Narayan and Rajaji respectively can be taken as examples of transcreation. P. Lal experimented with the art of transcreation in his earlier demonstration of *Great Sanskrit Plays into Modern Translation*. Sujit Mukherjee quotes the introductory note P. Lal's version of Shakuntala:

> Faced by such a variety of material, the translator must edit, reconcile and transmute: his job in many ways becomes largely a matter of transcreation.[6]

It is not possible to reproduce a text perfectly in another language—especially when the languages concerned are as distant as the Indian languages and English. In other words, the translator takes the role of a creator and translation when done well turns out to be 'new writing' or creative writing. I am inclined to agree with V.A. Shahane when he says:

> The value of Jussawalla's anthology (*i.e., New Writing in India*) consists, in part, in the extremely good selections he has made, which demonstrate not merely the literary values

but also the evolving concepts of social change and modernity as they affect creative sensitivity among Indian writers. The dynamics of social change is adequately reflected in these translation. The translations from the Urdu, *River of Life*, a novel by Qurratalain Hyder (by the author), from N. Pichamurti's Tamil Poem, *National Bird* (by R. Parthasarathy), from Vinda Karkandikar's Marathi Poem, *The Traitor* (by A.K. Ramanujan) are examples of expert rendering. These translations are not merely true to the original but also are highly sensitive, and aesthetically satisfying to the discriminating reader.[7] It is for this reason that Adil Jussawalla's *New Writing in India* and *Another India* co-edited by Nissim Ezekiel and Meenakshi Mukherjee can be justifiably called 'New Writings.' Speaking of Jussawalla's book V.A. Shahane praises Jussawalla for the first book of its kind. He writes that it is the first major attempt at translating modern Indian Writing into English and thereby giving the reader concrete examples of such writing and exposing him to wider literacy horizons.[8]

In the West *Bible* translation has taken the form of creative writing. The history of *Bible* translation is in a sense the history of western culture in microcosm. McGuire states that "the first translation of the complete *Bible* into English was the Wycliffe *Bible* produced between 1380 and 1384, which marked the start of great flowering of English *Bible* translations linked to changing attitudes to the role of the written text in the Church, that formed part of the developing reformation."[9] In the sixteenth century *Bible* was translated into several European languages. *The New Testament* was translated into Danisa in 1529, *The Great Bible* (1539) and *Bible* (1935) were translated with great success! In our century *Bible* has been translated into Indian languages with great success.

A translated text, it is said, is always a metatext or a text about a text. Popovic argues in course of an article "Translation as communication" about the nature of target text. "A target text is a metatext—not only because it imitates the source text but because it differs from the source text, and that the way of target text chooses to differ from the source text is indicative of the target text's conception of textuality."[10] The difference between the source text and the target text is a 'shift of expression.' This 'shift of expression' makes translation 'new writing' or creative writing.

The very act of translating has put him through the agonies and ecstasies of authorship. Hence, translation is a creative work and is its own reward. V.S. Naravane writes:

> No poet can turn into a translator unless he feels a subtle continuity between the work of original composition and the labour expended on interpreting the work of a kindred soul. In becoming a translator he does not cease to be personal. Through a remarkable paradox, the self-obliteration that translation involves itself becomes a means of self-expression. The translator has therefore been rightly described as 'a character in search of an author,' he finds the author first in another and then within himself.[11]

The translator's originality lies in an 'original' re-creation of the original. K. Chellappan has rightly suggested that 'this complex activity is not only an interlanguage event but also a cross-cultural communication because all linguistic signs are part of a larger social system of values. But good translations become creations or transcreations by exploiting this very gap of creativity.'[12] Translator is both—the reader and the writer. Since he creates something new, he should be accorded the status of a creative writer. In creative translation, several stages of back transformation can also be sudden resulting in a novel synthesis. Horst Frenz holds a similar view on the subject: "Two spheres of languages move closer together through the medium of the translator to fuse at the moment of the contact into a new form, a new Gestalt."[13] Thus, the translator transforms an SL text to a TL text by bringing a semantic compatibility between the two. This kind of transformation often takes place in the translation of poetry. In plain language, the translator creates something new in TL, taking the ingredients of the SL. This is perhaps what Steiner hints at when he says that "at its best the peculiar synthesis of conflict and complicity between a poem and its translation into another poem creates the impression of a 'third language,' or a medium of communicative energy which somehow reconciles both languages in a tongue deeper, more comprehensive than either."[14]

The concept of Translation as creative writing or new writing was in vogue both in the East and the West since long (*i.e.*, from the Puranic days and the time of the translation of the *Bible*). In the twentieth century with the advent of linguistics and criticism translation has not only been taken as 'New Writing' but literature three. Hence, translation has become creative—thanks to the concept of transcreation and transliteration. Therefore, the translator has outgrown the concept of being taken as a renderer of an SL text into a TL text and become a creator. In our technoelectronic age when everything has become creative (including creative cooking) translation too has become creative, much to the dismay of the critics of translation. Translation through transliteration takes words from one language (*i.e.*, SL) to another language (*i.e.*, TL) and thereby helps to broaden the vocabulary range of TL.

To conclude, I should say that in the light of developments in linguistics, translation has become creative. And this creative-aspect of translation gives a new status to it by making it 'New Writing.' Translation, without doubt, can be taken as creative writing or new writing.

## NOTES

1. Terence Hawkes, *Structuralism and Semiotics* (London: Methuen and Co. Ltd., 1977) 159.
2. Prema Nandakumar, "Translation: A Creative Process," *Cygnus* 2: 2 (1981): 65.
3. *Ibid.*, 61.
4. K. Ayyappa Paniker, "The Anxiety of Authenticity: Reflections on Literary Translation," *Critical Practice* 1: 2 (1994): 2.
5. Sujit Mukherjee, "Translation as New Writing," *Cygnus* 2: 2 (1981): 5-6.
6. *Ibid.*, 9.
7. V.A. Shahane, "Translation as Art," *Indian Literature* 26: 4 (1983): 13.
8. *Ibid.*, 12.
9. Susan Bassnett-McGuire, *Translation Studies* (New York: Routledge, 1991) 16.

10. *Michal Zellermayer*, "On Comments Made by Shifts in Translation," *Translation Across Cultures*. Ed. Gideon Toury (New Delhi: Bahri Publications Pvt. Ltd., 1987) 75-76.
11. Nandakumar, Quoted, 67.
12. K. Chellappan, "The Paradox of Transcreation," *Literature in Translation*. Ed. Pramod Talgeri and S.B. Verma (Bombay: Popular Prakashan, 1988) 159.
13. Horst Frenz, "The Art of Translation," *Comparative Literature: Method and Perspective* ed. Newton, P. Stallknecher and Horst Frenz (Carbondale and Edwardaville, Southern Illionis University Press, 1961) 120.
14. George Steiner, ed., "Introduction," *Poem into Poem* (Penguin Books, 1970) 29.

# 6

# Translation as Linguistic Bridge-Building

Taking a cue from an anthropologist Malinowski, J.R. Firth thought of translation as a kind of bridge-building languages or linguistic bridge-building. Translation without the medium of language is unthinkable. Therefore, of all the arts, literature alone is faced with the problem of translation for it uses different languages as its medium of expression. We do not think of translation in the field of fine arts such as music, dance, painting or even architecture or sculpture where the medium is not language. In non-literacy translation, the medium is again language. Human beings communicate among themselves through language. But different peoples speak different languages in different parts of the world. That is why we need translation for the purpose of communication among people of different races, cultures and faiths all over the world. And translation becomes a kind of linguistic bridge-building.

The writer, his reader and work belong to one language and the translator, his reader and translation belong to another language (of course, the translator knows both the languages). What happens in translation is that the SL text gets substituted and the result is that the TL text is born. In other words, translation is a journey from one language to another. Since language is a code or system of signs, the translator decodes the SL text and recodes it in the TL text. Thus, in translation, decoding and recoding, destructuring and re-structuring take place. Since languages differ in form and structure, translation acts as a kind of linguistic bridge-building between two languages and cultures.

Translation is a two-dimensional process—not unidirectional as some people take it to be. It depends on the interpretation of verbal signs in the same language and also outside the language (*i.e.*, in another language). We know that the meaning of any linguistic sign is its translation into some further, alternative sign, especially a sign 'in which it is more fully developed.'[1] Roman Jakobson further elaborates this point in the following words:

> We distinguish three ways of interpreting a verbal sign: it may be translated into other signs of the same language, into another language, or into another, non-verbal system of symbols. These three kinds of translation are to be differently labelled:
>
> (1) Intralingual translation or rewording is an interpretation of verbal signs by means of other signs of the same language.
>
> (2) Interlingual translation or translation proper is an interpretation of verbal signs by means of some other language.
>
> (3) Intersemiotic translation or transmutation is an interpretation of verbal signs by means of signs of non-verbal sign systems.
>
> The intralingual translation of a word uses either another, more or less synonymous word or resorts to a circumlocution. Yet synonymy, as a rule, is not complete equivalence: for example, "every celibate is a bachelor, but not every bachelor is a celibate." A word or an indiomatic phrase-word, briefly a code-unit of the highest level, may be fully interpreted only by means of an equivalent combination of code-units, *i.e.*, a message referring to this code-unit: "every bachelor is an unmarried man, and every unmarried man is a bachelor," or "every celibate is bound not to marry, and everyone who is bound not to marry is a celibate."
>
> Likewise, on the level of interlingual translation, there is ordinarily no full equivalence between code-units, while messages may serve as adequate interpretations of alien code-units or messages. The English word "cheese" cannot be completely

identified with its standard Russian heteronym "cup," because cottage cheese is a cheese but not a cup. Russians says: UPHHECH CUPY H TBOPORY, "bring cheese and [*sic*] cottage cheese." In standard Russian, the food made of pressed curds is called cup only if ferment is used.

Most frequently, however, translation from one language into another substitutes messages in one language not for separate code-units but for entire message in some other language. Such a translation is a reported speech; the translator records and transmits a message received from another source. Thus translation involves two equivalent messages in two different codes.[2]

Take for instance the translation of certain culture based words from one language into another language which are linguistically and culturally different. And that will show translation as a kind of bridge-building languages. Many Indian food items will defy translation into English. Bertrand Russell's example of 'cheese' is well-known. Similarly many Oriya food items like 'Pakhal' ('watered rice'), 'Kanji' (a kind of 'Dal' prepared from watered rice), 'Sukua' (dry-fish), etc. cannot be intelligible to a non-native speaker or an Englishman. These words are linguistic or semiotic fact in the sameway, as Roman Jakobson pleads for certain items in the following lines:

> The meaning of the words "cheese," "apple," "nectar," "acquaintance," "but," "mere," and of any word or phrase whatsoever is definitely a linguistic—or to be more precise and less narrow—a semiotic fact. Against those who assign meaning (signature) not to the sign, but to the thing itself, the simplest and truest argument would be that nobody has ever smelled or tasted the meaning of "cheese" or of "apple." There is no signarum without signum. The meaning of the word "cheese" cannot be inferred from a non-linguistic acquaintance with cheddar or with camembert without the assistance of the verbal code. An array of linguistic signs is needed to introduce an unfamiliar word. Mere pointing will not teach us whether "cheese" is the name of the given specimen, or of any box of camembert, or of camembert in general or of any cheese, any milk product, any food, any refreshment, or perhaps any box irrespective of contents.

> Finally, does a word simply name the thing in question, or does it imply a meaning such as offering, sale, prohibition, or malediction. (Pointing actually may mean malediction: in some cultures, particularly in Africa, it is an ominous gesture).[3]

J.C. Catford gave a clear statement of theoretical formulations about the linguistics of translation in his book, *A Linguistic Theory of Translation*. He holds that since translation is a linguistic act, any theory of translation must emerge from linguistics. He writes: "Translation is an operation performed on languages, a process of substituting a text in one language for a text in another. Clearly then, any theory of translation must draw upon a theory of language—a general linguistic theory."[4]

Since translation is based on linguistics, we have to take into account Saussure concept of 'signs, signifier and signified.'[5] Thus, Derrida writes:

> Within the limits of its possibility, or its apparent possibility, translation practices the difference between signified and signifier. But, if this difference is never pure, translation is less so, and a notion of transformation must be substituted for the notion of translation, a regulated transformation of one language by another, or one text by another. We shall not have and never have had to deal with some 'transfer' of pure signifieds that the signifying instrument—or 'vehicle'—would leave virgin and intact, from one language to another, or within one and the same language.[6]

Since translation is a transformation from SL text into TL text, we have to take note of the surface meaning as well as the deep meaning. The surface meaning is normally taken into account while the structure is more or less static. It is stated rightly that when surface meaning is sought to be transferred through equivalence, its surface cannot be changed. We know that no two languages have equal or identical structures. That explains the inadequacy of translation. Certain English words which defy gender classifications create problems for Indian translators. That is because in Indian languages particularly in Oriya the gender difference of certain words are clearly shown, unlike that of the equivalent English words. For example, English words like 'student,' 'teacher,' 'worker,' 'doctor,' 'engineer,' 'legislator,' 'professor,' etc. do not show any gender distinction while in Oriya we have two equivalent words for each English word mentioned here. Sentences like 'My teacher punished me,' 'I hired a worker,' 'The number of students of this class is 50,' 'My uncle gave me ₹ 500/-,' 'My cousin helped me to go abroad,' etc. will be ambiguous and their translation into Oriya needs further explanation or elaboration. This is because the gender is essential in translation into Oriya. Otherwise, these sentences will be complicated and inadequate when rendered into Oriya. Since the information needed by the Oriya grammatical form is different from that of the English grammatical form, one faces quite distinct sets of choice situations. For example, the all encompassing simple English word 'you' has three corresponding Oriya forms 'Tu,' 'Tume' and 'Apaṇa.' 'Tu' refers to a second person, with whom the speaker has a greater degree of intimacy and 'Tume' refers to the second person with whom the speeker has formal relationship and may be equal status. And 'Apana' refers to a person whom the speaker holds in high esteem and who is senior to the speaker. In nutshell, in Oriya 'Tu' is an affectionate address to the second person, 'Tume' is a formal address to the second person and 'Apana' is a reverential address to the second person by the speaker.

As stated above languages which are structurally different create linguistic problems and need some kind of linguistic bridge-building to make the translation viable. In English we use simple present tense to convey things happening at the moment (or to indicate present status) but in Oriya we use present progressive tense to state the samething. For example, we say, 'I am working at a college,' "I am suffering from fever," "I am feeling cold," 'I am loving her,' etc. in Oriya, the equivalent English sentences will be 'I work at a college,' "I suffer from fever," "I feel cold," and "I love her," etc. The use of progressive tense in English by Oriya speakers create ungrammaticalness because of the gravitational pull of the mother tongue. Take for instance, the following sentences: 'Mu Sabu Dekhuchi' ('I am seeing everything' instead of 'I see everything'). 'Mu Sabu Sunuchi' ('I am hearing everything' instead of 'I hear everything'), 'Mu Sabu bujhabujhi karuchi' ('I am overseeing or looking after everything' instead of 'I oversee everything' or 'I look after everything')—these sentences create ungrammaticalness in English if rendered literally. Again we use the present tense form of primary auxiliary 'have' in a sentence 'I have seen her last week' in Oriya instead of 'I had seen her last week.'

As Benjamin Lee Whorf has rightly suggested that "facts are unlike to speakers whose language background provides for unlike formulation of them."[7] For example, the words 'incest,' and 'morality' mean differently to persons belonging to different linguistic and cultural background. For example, to say that one wants to marry his or her cousin in coastal districts of Orissa is to be accused of incest. But in the southern districts of Orissa and in South India one invariably marries one's cousin. Similarly, Roman Jakobson gives an interesting account of the linguistic aspect of translation in the following way:

> In the first years of the Russian revolution there were fanatic visionaries who argued in Soviet periodicals for a radical revision of traditional language and particularly for the weeding out of such misleading expressions as "sunrise" or "sunset." Yet we still use this Ptolemaic imagery without implying a rejection of Copernican doctrine, and we can easily transform our customary talk about the rising and setting sun into a picture of the earth's rotation simply because any sign is translatable into a sign in which it appears to us more fully developed and precise.

A faculty of speaking a given language implies a faculty of talking about this language. Such a "metalinguistic" operation permits revision and redefinition of the vocabulary used. The complementarily of both levies—object-language and metalanguage—was brought out by Nicls Bohr all well-defined experimental evidence must be expressed in ordinary language, "in which the practical use of every word stands in complementary relation to attempts of its strict definition."

All cognitive experience and its classification is conveyable in any existing language. Whenever there is deficiency, terminology may be qualified and amplified loanwords or loan-translations, neologisms or semantic shifts, and finally, by circumlocutions. Thus in the newborn literary language of the Northeast Siberian Chukchees, "screw" is rendered as "rotating nail," "steel" as "hard iron," "tin" as "thin iron," "chalk" as "writing soap," "watch" as "hammering heart." Even seemingly contradictory circumlocutions, like "electrical horse-car," the first Russian name of the horseless street car, or "flying steamship" (jena paragot), the Koryak term for the airplane, simply designate the electrical analogue of the house-car and the flying analogue of the steamer and do not impede communication, just as there is no semantic "noise" and disturbance in the double oxymoron—"cold beef-and-pork hot dog."[8]

Polyglots and linguists say that for every word in any one language, there is not another word accurately equivalent to it in every other language. It is within common knowledge that words in one language have dialectal variations. That means the same word means differently in two different dialects within the same language. If an SL text contains passages in a dialect other than the unmarked dialect, the translator may have to choose an equivalent dialect in the target language. Regional dialects not only vary but create new meanings. Let's take the case of Oriya language. It contains three standard dialects—Cuttacki, Sambalpuri and Berhampuri. 'Reja' in Sambalpur dialect means 'girl' but in Cuttacki dialect it means 'change coins.' Such kind of words create problems for the translator. Apart from dialects of various kinds such as social, geographical and prestige, the translator also encounters the problems of register, style and various changes of language in the process of translating a text from SL to TL.

As we know that Register, Style and Mode are varieties of language connected with the immediate situation of utterance. Register implies a variety correlated with the official and social role of the performer in a given situation. Like dialects, registers, can be explained with lesser or greater specificity; thus, while in English a general scientific register may be identified, sub-registers within this may also be differentiated. Register markers are mainly lexical and grammatical, particularly grammatical-statistical forms such as the high frequency of passive verbs, and the low frequency of the pronouns in scientific register of English.

During the translation process, the choice of an appropriate register in the target language is often significant. Here, if there is no equivalent register in the target language, untranslatability may occur. One of the problems of rendering scientific texts into certain languages such as Hindi and Oriya our National and State language respectively, is that of finding, or creating an equivalent scientific register.

Style implies a variety which correlates with the number and nature of the addressees and the relationship of the performer to them. Styles differ along a scale which may be defined as formal or informal. The markers of styles may be lexical, grammatical or phonological. The translatability of styles depends on the existence of an equivalent style in the target language.

The translation equivalent must be established between the varieties as such, and the specific markers may be distinct in the texts of the source language and the target language. The equivalence is based on similarities of situation—substance—merely, those which are stylistically essential in one language may not be in another. It is easy for an English young man to address his father in casual style; on the other hand an oriental young man may have to use honorific forms in the same situation. Both respect and affection may be there in the situation, but respect may not be stylistically essential for the English son, while it is essential for the Asian son. While in English we use the prefix 'Mr.' before senior's (for that matter before any male name) name, in India we use the suffix 'ji' after senior's name. For instance we address Nehru as Mr. Nehru in English but Nehruji in Hindi.

A number of approaches to the theory of translation available now is not holistic. About the linguistic theory of translation Udaya Narayan Singh says, "Linguists identified the translation theory with analysis of semantic and grammatical operations. In the beginning, they took it for granted that the Aristotelian approach of signs containing meaning was true—a position that was seriously challenged by the American structural linguists in the first part of this century. These structuralists rather viewed translator's aim as creation of a language structure which would evoke the same reaction in the target language reader as the original had in the source language readers. Firth and his followers on the other hand, talked in terms of linguistic equivalence and the fit of the translated fragment into the same social context as that of the original. Notice that here it is taken for granted that translation was a mere extension and application of linguistics. The question that one can legitimately ask is this: can a translation theory merely aim at description and validation of lexical and grammatical manipulations meant to attain the semantic equivalent? Can the wider question of discourse be neglected by concentrating merely on grammar and lexicon? Are the subjective and objective content of the linguistic sign as consistent as they are usually thought to be? What is the social implication of the Saussurian dichotomy of 'signification' and value? Some linguists talked about 'adequacy' of a translated text. This I consider to be potentially dangerous weapon to knock down any attempt to translate because it is an undefinable concept at the mercy of intellectuals."[9]

Translator, not being the original author (for the work in hand is never his own) takes unto himself the task of bridge-building between the mind of the author and the mind of the reader or between an SL text and the TL text. Since the lexical items vary from language to language, the translation should act as a linguistic bridge-building. B.N. Patnaik gives an interesting account of lexical items in Oriya and English in the following words:

> Oriya does not have two lexical items corresponding to "assassinate" and "kill." The lexical items 'mariba' and 'hatyakariba' (both corresponding to "kill") belong to two different styles; the first, to the colloquial, the second, to the formal, and these are not really directly concerned with the importance of the target. Interestingly, there are some lexical items in Oriya which express the sense of "die" and these indeed are sensitive to whether the dead person is the object of veneration or not. If he is not, then the appropriate word

> is 'mariba' (not to be confused with 'mariba' "kill") in which the first vowel is / a:/, not /a/), but if he is, then the appropriate items would be dehatyaga kariba ("give up the body"). Swargabasa Kariba (left for heavenly abode) and the like.[10]

Similarly English words 'corpse,' 'deadbody,' 'mortal remains' do not mean the Oriya word 'Saba' alone for they have different connotations. The translation must be done in such a way as not to hurt the sentiments of the TL speakers. That means, translation should not be only a mere rendering of an SL text into a TL text but it should bridge the linguistic gap between two languages and the speakers of both the languages. For example if a speech by Nehru in Hindi is to be translated into English or a speech by Churchil in English is to be translated into Hindi, then the translator should take care to do it in such a way as to sound original (*i.e.*, Nehru's speech when translated into English should retain his style and so also Churchil's speech his own style).

The process of translation begins with the analysis of the source language text, in terms of lexis, grammar as well as discourse. This is followed by, as Maya Pandit has rightly pointed out that, "the process of translation involves analysis of the source language text, in terms of lexis, grammar as well as discourse. This is followed by the process of transferring this deep structure conglomeration of meaning to the TL and finally, the message is restructured in terms of the signs of the target language. In this process, an attempt is made to preserve, as far as possible, the invariant information with respect to the given system of reference. The translation of even a single word involves the problems of the semantic range and distribution of that term in the language, the syntagmatic and paradigmatic relationships the word has with the other terms in the language, the social context of its use and the function it has at the level of discourse. Thus, the equivalence will have to be established on the linguistic level (on the levels of lexis and grammar), stylistic level and pragmatic level. These levels have a hierarchical relationship. The most important is the pragmatic level because the pragmatic considerations would modify and even define the equivalence at the other two levels. Equivalence would result from a consideration of the relationship existing between signs at all these levels. Thus, the question of establishing equivalence cannot be considered in a cultural vacuum. It will have to be treated in the framework of the specific spatio-temporal-cultural context within which a text is produced in the source language and its translation in the target language. It may thus be argued that a text is not totally autonomous. It is, in fact, a structure made up of signs which are in opposition to the signs within the text and without it. The consideration of signs and their structures will have to be done with respect to the functional role the various structural elements play in the text. These may include the choice of various artistic procedures, the styles, the registers of language utilized and the various tonalities employed by the author. The theory of intertextuality will have a great deal of importance in this context."[11]

In conclusion to this chapter, I would like to say that the reader of a translation belongs to, as a matter of fact, another language and may be to another culture. The author of the original work belongs to a different language and culture. This dichotomy leads to a gap between the pragmatics of the original text on the one hand and that of the translated text on the other. Thus, translation should aim at bridging the gap between the pragmatic differences as reflected in the systems of the two languages concerned and more importantly to bridge the gap between the specific contexts which depend on certain linguistic, historical and socio-cultural circumstances. Translation, when succeeds in bridge-building languages (SL and TL), reads like an original work. Perhaps, that is the true test of translation.

## NOTES

1. John Dewey, 'Pierce's Theory of Linguistic Signs, Thought, and Meaning,' *The Journal of Philosophy* 43 (1946): 97.
2. Roman Jakobson, "On Linguistic Aspects of Translation," *On Translation*. Ed. R.A. Brower (New York: Oxford University Press, 1968) 233.
3. *Ibid.*, 232.
4. J.C. Catford, *A Linguistic Theory of Translation* (London: Oxford University Press, 1965) VII.

5. Gayatri Spivak, *Tr. of Grammatology* (Baltimore: OUP) LXXXVII.
6. *Ibid.*, LXXXVI.
7. Benjamin Lee Whorf, *Language. Thought and Reality* (Cambridge, Mass, 1956) 235.
8. Jakobson 234-35.
9. Udaya Narayan Singh, "Translation Theory: An Attempt at Understanding," *International Journal of Translation* 1: 2 (1989): 73.
10. B.N. Patnaik, "Conceptual and Linguistic Decisions in Generation," *International Journal of Translation* 2: 2 (July-Dec., 1990): 16.
11. Maya Pandit, "The Problems of Translation," *The Literary Criticism* 22: 2 (1987): 58-59.

# 7

# Translation as Nation Building

We are on the threshold of the twenty-first century. In the present context of national development, translation is considered as an important aspect and component of language learning. As the world has become a 'global village' and 'Internet' has facilitated the communication system, the role of translation has widened beyond expectation. At the national level, translation helps in bringing out national integration (more so, in multilingual countries like India, France, Canada, etc.) and at the international level it helps in improving good relations among neighbouring countries and bi-lateral relationships. In a way, translation helps the people in their effort at nation building, and establishing the national identity.

Paul St. Pierre reiterates the concept of translation as nation building in the following words:

> The importance of translation can be located in the fact that translation brings the readers, writers, and critics of one nation into contact with those of others, not only in the field of literature, but in all areas of human development: science and philosophy, medicine, political science, law and religion, to name but a few. Translation, in this way, plays an essential role in determining how a nation establishes its identity in terms of others, be this through *opposition* to foreign influences, through *assimilation* or "*naturalization*" of the foreign whereby differences are erased to as great a degree possible, or through *imitation* of another, usually dominant culture. These are all different strategies of translation, becoming possibilities at different moments in

> history and underlining the various types of relations between nations which can exist. There is, thus, a particularly strong interconnection between translation and the constitution of national identity, and the study of translation can be useful—as I will attempt to show later in this paper—in determining the nature of this national identity, and the nature of the relations one nation institutes with others. Seen in this light, translation is a social practice with a definite role to play within a given society, serving in a sense as a form of selection process restricting, conditioning, and in any case modulating cultural immigration. Through translation nations define themselves and in doing so they define others.[1]

In a multi-lingual and multi-cultural country like India, translation of words is of paramount importance for exchange of ideas and thoughts among people belonging to different regions, languages and culture. Without translation it is well-neigh impossible for the people of India to communicate among themselves. For mass information and technical know-how translation from one regional language into another or to the national language, Hindi and Pan-Indian language, English is not only necessary but inevitable. Two important modern Indian English writers, Amitav Ghosh and Dilip Chitre have emphasized this point and suggested that translation is highly essential in our country. Amitav Ghosh writes:

> And the thing about translation is that there is no way around it. In a country as multilingual as ours, unless you have really good translations, you are doomed.[2]

Translation is not only a vehicle of reaching out the people but it serves as a bridge among regional languages and people of India. Dilip Chitre writes:

> Even as an independent practicing poet, I live in the Postmodern world transformed by translation. This is my predicament as a writer. I have to build a bridge within myself between India and Europe or else I become a fragmented person.[3]

The translation of literatures in India has assumed a special status in our century. The ancient Indian literary heritage which is to be found in languages like Sanskrit, Prakrit and Apbransha, etc. can be preserved and even rescued only through translation into English and several regional languages. Indian literature which is a cover term for all regional literatures of India including Hindi literature, Sanskrit literature and Indian English literature, can reach all the people of India only through translation. In other words, it is through translation that one regional literature can reach the people of another region of the country speaking a different language. In this context, V.A. Shahane makes a pertinent point in the following passages:

> The relevance of translations from Indian regional languages into English to our contemporary cultural ethos and literary culture must at once be recognized without any hesitation whatever. Indian culture is a mosaic of many sub-cultures covering different linguistic regions and their regional literatures and lifestyles. Indian culture is more like a salad of different vegetables and organic growth rather than a 'melting pot' in which different ethnic components swiftly melt away and lose their identity. The theory of the growth of Indian civilization can best be symbolized in this beautiful image of the salad rather than in the image of the "cauldron." American social historians and sociologists (Nathan Glazer notably, among them) have advanced the theory of the 'melting pot' of American civilization (in Beyond the Melting Pot) which suggests that different ethnic cultures of Europe and other continents have submerged and finally assumed the form and shape of American civilization. This theory has, of course, been challenged by many other historians in the recent past. That apart, Indian society has always been multi-racial, multi-religious, multi-subcultural and multi-lingual and therefore very much like a salad.
>
> If this 'salad' image of our civilization is accepted as a basic truth, the existence of various Indian regional literatures can at once be accepted as significant layers of our social structure and literary culture. In fact, no student could be considered to have understood present-day Indian literary culture without coming to terms with the elements of this 'salad,' the organic subgrowths of our civilization. How can Indo-

> English literature (which is still the medium of creative expression of a small English educated minority) claim to voice the urges of a vast majority of Indian people and be the instrument of their creative expression unless it encompasses within it the moving spirit of all these regional sub-cultures and their literatures? The relations between the creative writers of Indo-Anglian literature and those of regional Indian literatures should be based on mutual exchange and partnership in shared values of a composite, multifarious culture. A spirit of cooperation, co-existence, and coordination, rather than of isolation and confrontation, should govern our multilingual literary culture.[4]

In order to translate one regional Indian literature into either English or any other regional literature of the country, the translator should have an inwardness not only with both SL and TL but with their cultures. Unless the translator has the knowledge of both the languages and cultures, he will not be able to translate the regional literatures into English or other Indian languages with authenticity. I am inclined to agree with the following remarks of Cay Dollerup:

> A good transmission demands that the mediator (a) has a thorough knowledge of both source and target-language culture and language, (b) is familiar with a large number of different disciplines, fields, and human activities, (c) has common sense, (d) is in tune with the message to be transmitted, (e) strives to understand all statements in their contexts, (f) is consciously aware of things which must obviously be checked and has a hunch, or flair, for identifying others which need to be checked, (g) and is conscientious so that problems are solved as well as possible instead of skipped.[5]

Translation helps in the process of nation building in our country. The language of our administrative communication at the national level (*i.e.*, by the Central Government) is done either through the official language, or in English. It needs to be translated into more than 20 regional languages for the benefit of the people of several states. Similarly the language of the court is either English or Hindi and the judgement is delivered in one of these two languages. Thereafter the judgement is translated into regional language for the benefit of the common people. For administrative and judiciary purposes, translation is obligatory in India. For the promotion of commerce, trade and industry in our country, we make use of translation. In the modern world, the need for translation is greater than ever before.

In the international field we need to translate for bi-lateral talks, and for discussion at the UN and all other international meetings and deliberations. Without translation, it is impossible for world leaders to communicate among themselves. Hence, translation is taken as nation building.

Translation of world classics into several other languages of the world helps in enriching the target languages. Apart from well-known epics of the world, great authors like Tolstoy, and Shakespeare, continue to be translated into several languages. New trends in literature come through translation. The two great epics of India, *The Ramayana* and *The Mahabharata* have been translated into almost all the regional languages of India. That helped, the creation of Pan-Indian ethos. National myths like 'Laxman Rekha' (*i.e.,* the lines drawn by Laxman, in *the Ramayana* to warn Sita), and 'Bhisma Pratigya' (the oath of Bhisma in *the Mahabharata,* an oath never to be broken) have stirred the minds of the Indians and these myths are available to our people through translations. G.N. Devy gives an interesting account of the role of translation in the Indian situation.

In the Indian context literary translations can be divided into three types: (i) those interested in preserving the ancient literary heritage, (ii) those interested in 'Westernising' Indian languages and literature, and (iii) those interested in 'nationalizing' literature in mordern Indian languages. In correspondence with the different objectives of these three types, their mode of operation differs.

The modern Indian languages originating in Sanskrit have a long history of translations from Sanskrit. Their literary traditions are full of instances of renderings of the Sanskrit epics and other literature. Many of these languages have one or the other illustrious translation at the very beginning of the literary tradition. *Jnanesvari* in Marathi is one such example. These translations were made without any inhibition, and they rarely maintained a word-for-word, line-for-line discipline. The categories useful for the study of these translations are not 'the TL and the SL' or 'the mother tongue and the other tongue.' The poets/writers attempting vernacular renderings of Sanskrit texts treated both the languages as their 'own' languages. They had a sense of possession in respect of the Sanskrit heritage. But in translating the Sanskrit texts they sought to liberate the scriptures from the monopoly of a restricted class of people. Hence, their translations became a means of reorganizing the entire society. No theory with an exclusively linguistic orientation can be adequate to understand the magnitude of translation activity in India.

With the advent of the British power in India, and with the spread of English education, a new value-structure emerged in India. In this value structure everything British was considered to be inherently good. In literature, the most obvious consequence of this colonial value scheme was an indiscriminate institutionalization of English literature. During the nineteenth century it was highly fashionable in India to translate all the sundry works of English literature. In that period Shakespeare was translated as were Scott and Bunyan. The basic idea behind such an indiscriminate translation activity was that more translations from English will strengthen Indian languages. When the translation activity in a given language grows in a proportion that is completely out of tune with the natural growth of that language, the sub-system of language within which translations operate comes to occupy the centre-stage. Most of the translations from English into Indian languages were in prose. Therefore, the prose styles in modern Indian languages have acquired an inevitable texture and tone of translation language. They are less supple than what they need to be. Today, when an Indian writes prose in an Indian language, the reader often suspects the existence of an undesirable gap between the written prose and the spoken language. This colonial legacy is so firmly rooted in contemporary Indian literary culture that often we find Indians making a naïve claim that literary prose is a positive and original contribution made by the British to Indian culture. The purely linguistic and neutral theories of translation would be inadequate to understand the politically motivated colonial translation activity. In order to arrive at a satisfactory analysis of the Indian translation activity initiated by colonialism, the linguistic theories need to be supported by an awareness of the colonial discourse.[6]

Not only in India but in other parts of the world where multilingualism is a reality like France, Canada and Switzerland, translation plays a vital role in nation building. Movements in literature, art and trends in political opinion sails from country to country through translation. The practitioners of translation face great difficulties in translating different culture contexts and linguistic codes and therefore, to translate a text of one country into another is to transform it. In the colonial era translation was considered to be power. The colonizer used translation as a means to oppress the colonized and the colonized used translation to maintain the indigenous culture and tradition. Paul St. Pierre gives an interesting account of this problem in the following words:

> To translate, I have already said, means to situate oneself in terms of another defined as "other" and the way in which such a relation is realized can run the gamut from complete denial of the alterity of the culture translated to slavish imitation. When French works were translated into English in the eighteenth century, for example, Englishness was constructed through a coming to terms with what was the dominant culture at the time—the French culture—and such confrontations were seen even in military terms. Thus J. Ozell writes in his letter to Lord Halifax which heads the translation of the works of Boileau (1712): "...it has been thought by some as rash an attempt to translate this French Author, as for an English General to attack an Army of theirs.... But certain it is that the French Genius may be match'd (if not surpass'd) in both, the Pen as well as the Sword; whatever exalted Notions to the contrary some amongst us may have, who cou'd relish Slavery itself, if it were but French." The second ambiguity is thus that

through translation difference is at one and the same time held at bay (through the process of "naturalization" or "reterritorialization" inherent to all translation, though this can take place to varying degrees) and yet becomes that which serves to define 'similarity' (that which each citizen has in common with every other fellow citizen, and which serves to distinguish him from those of other nations). And these relations between nations are marked by relations of power, although never, it should be noted, in a simple, unidirectional way. Thus, while colonizers may attempt to use translation as a tool of oppression, by forcing the translated language to conform to the mold of that into which it is translated, thereby, as Vicente Rafael has noted in *Contracting Colonialism,* "articulating the general outlines of subjugation," the colonized can also make use of translation as a way of maintaining their distinct cultural identity. This is what Rafael describes as being the case in The Philippines, where the Tagalogs resisted the Spanish attempts to establish a hierarchy of languages (Latin-Castillian-Tagalog) and a hierarchy of societies, by marking the differences separating them from the Spaniards. It is also the case, as we shall see, of the role of translation in the context of theatre in Quebec. Thus whereas translation can indeed be a tool with a strong political dimension, it is not an unambiguous tool since it can serve both the dominator and the dominated: the first by creating a certain transparency, which—it should be noted—is always in their favour (and not only on the level of language), and the second by preserving the other as other, the structures of colonization as external, imported and historical. Thus when France dominated Europe at the beginning of the eighteenth century, translations into French naturalized foreign texts to as great a degree as possible, and translation coincided with French imperial destiny and designs, conquering foreign parts and constantly extending the realm. In the late-twentieth century, however, France's role has changed, and translation into French now has a quite different function: that of preserving the French language and culture, rather than of

> confirming and extending their dominance. In both cases translation involves a hierarchy and relations of power, but these relations involve at different moments in time the interests of different groups. We will find this also to be true of the role of translation within the Canadian context.[7]

In the postcolonial phase the onus for continuing in English is ours alone. It is necessary for the purpose of translation. In India it is imperative on the part of a person of one state to translate his words in the native language into either English or Hindi (mostly English) to communicate himself to another person belonging to another regional language. Translation bridges the cultural and linguistic gap between two languages. As Susan Daniel rightly says:

> Translation as a means of setting right the depletion of languages, or as an attempt to rediscover a lost erotics, sounds worthy of espousal, especially when it vouches for protection against erosion and alienation. This need not apply to former times and literature alone. The replenishment the English language is receiving in the hands of third world writing today, one tends to believe, will continue for some more time, and translators will have to probe their filiation in the shifting psychic boundaries as well.... Translation as testimony of a precolonial self is now the conventicle of new directions that need to be explored. Lofty considerations affirming the primacy of consciousness and the teleology implicit in that primacy apart, what is of special interest is the manner in which translations function as a means of regeneration, as a process of assimilation intensified and enriched through contiguity with others.[8]

Translation is power and it is a means to propagate religion and culture. *The Authorized Version of the Bible* influenced and converted millions of people into Christianity in the British colonies. Hence, translation can be taken as power and it is linked with national identity. The role of translation in nation-building cannot be lost sight of.

## NOTES

1. Paul St. Pierre, "Translation and National Identity," an unpublished paper sent to me.
2. Amitav Ghosh, *Indian Express,* March 20, 1994.
3. Dilip Chitre, 'Editor's Note,' *Critical Practice* 1: 2 (1994): 3.
4. V.A. Shahane, "Translation as Art," *Indian Literature* 26: 4 (July-August, 1983): 9-10.
5. Cay Dollerup, "Control of Interlingual Mediation in Practice: Denmark as a Case Study," *Multilingua* 6: 2 (1987): 175-76.
6. G.N. Devy, "Translation Theory: An Indian Perspective," *In Another Tongue* (Madras: MacMillan, 1995) 149-50.
7. Pierre 4-5.
8. Susan Daniel, "Walking the Boundaries: the Translation Exercise," *Anuvada* 2: 2 (1991): 12.

# 8

# The Limits of Translation

The practice of translation is not without its limitation. The first difficulty lies in the opposition between similarity and difference among words in SL and TL. Translation aims at producing a text which can stand in a relation of equivalence to another text. Since linguistic codes and cultural contexts are not 'equipollent,' to translate a text is to transform it.

The first point that comes to mind is that what should be the length of translation. Should it be longer or shorter than the original? In case of free translation, when translation becomes a paraphrase, it becomes much longer than the original. Moreover, the number of words do not remain the same in both the languages—SL and TL. For instance, only nine words in English 'The quick brown fox jumps over the lazy dog' (Theodore Savory's example) make use of all the 26 letters of English alphabet. But I don't think any Indian language can use all the letters of its alphabet with the help of nine words—not atleast, Oriya.

The notion that for every word in any one language there is another word accurately equivalent to it in every other language is no longer tenable. For example, a simple word 'love' in English has a host of equivalent words in Oriya and most of the Indian languages. Similarly, erotic vocabulary is very poor in English, while Indian languages (particularly Sanskrit), have a rich erotic vocabulary. Julius Caesar's famous words: "Veni, Vidi, Vici" are translated into English as, "I reached the country after long matches, I surveyed the position before undertaking military action, and in this I successfully subjugated the defenders."[1]

Since words are different from language to language, the question arises: when is a translation not a translation? In other words, what are the limits of translation? The limits of translation are many and therefore, it is necessary to find out when and where translation fails to deliver the good. The first limitation of translation is its failure to convey the jargons of one language through another language. Let us begin with the limits of jargon translation.

Jargons of one language cannot be easily translated into another language. In everyday language and speech we sometimes come across professional language and jargon coming together. Specialists speak in technical language which is very difficult to translate and one is left with no alternative than to transliterate the register of a technical person. As Arthur Koestler rightly points out that "Needless to say, technical communications addressed to specialists must employ technical language; but even here the overloading with jargon, the tortuous and cramped style, are largely a matter of conforming to fashion" (*The Act of Creation,* 265). And it is difficult to translate such communication into another language.

Alan Duff in course of an article titled, "Professional language or Jargon?" defines international jargon as follows:

> This jargon is characterized by: repetition, redundancy (*i.e.,* too many words), mixed metaphor, and above all—by in clarity of thought. It is Lego-language, made up of ready-shaped blocks which can be stuck together to build sentences of readymade meaning, just as the little plastic blocks themselves can without changing their form—be used as doors, windows, areoplane wings or wigwam flaps.

Critical terms are difficult to translate into another language. For example, terms like 'romanticism,' 'classicism,' 'structuralism,' 'deconstruction,' 'objective correlative,' 'auditory imagination,' 'affective fallacy,' etc. cannot be translated into Indian languages without footnotes. It is better to transliterate these terms into Indian languages. Thus, one major limitation of translation is that it cannot successfully convey or transform professional jargons, critical terms and idioms from one language to another language.

Faithfulness in translation is indispensible and when it is abandoned, translation turns out to be a virtual paraphrase. When translators have taken freedom to the limit, others have turned it to licence. If unlimited freedom is given to the translator, translation ceases to be translation, it becomes a transcript or an adaptation. Sometimes, translation is based on 'illusory equivalence' (Theodore Savory's phrase) for it is thought that every word of a language has an equivalent word in another language. In case of cultural expressions, the limitation of translation becomes clear and glaring, for cultural idioms are hard to translate and restrict translatability. Theodore Savory hints at the limits of translation in the following words:

> Troubles of a different kind arise from gaps in languages, which cannot be filled by translating because for a word that may be quite familiar in one language there is no equivalent in another. Probably the first example that will occur to many is the failure of French to provide a word for 'home.' 'I shall go home,' says the Englishman; and the Frenchman: 'F'irai chez moi.' "This is my home," says the Englishman on arrival; but the Frenchman can get no nearer than Voild ma maison, or mon logis or ma demeure, all words whose primary significance is that contained in the Englishman's 'house' or 'residence.' So, too, there is no English word for the French menu or for the Latin word augur and no Latin word for the English word 'premier.'[2]

Translation of rhythm and rhyme schemes in poetry into another is almost impossible. In case of poetry, translation is restricted to ideas only, not to the form—for form varies from language to language. The musicality of a poem along with its technical virtuosity cannot be translated. This is a serious limitation of translation.

Humours based on a particular culture and jokes of a particular community or place, are hard to translate and even if they are translated they lose their force, vigour and appeal in the target language. Metaphor, pun and irony severely limit the degree of translatability. Superstition, folk-belief and myth affect the role of translation. For example, certain numbers which are considered to be inauspicious in one culture becomes normal in another, and that limits the scope of translation.

Languages differ from each other, the way they are structured—phonological, syntactic, lexico-semantic and so on. That is why languages are not all equivalent in expressive power. Take for example, two languages English and Oriya—the former is SVO language and the latter is SOV language. A sentence in English 'I gave you a book' cannot be translated into Oriya as 'Mu dheithili tumaku gotia bahi' for that will create unnaturalness in Oriya and it should be 'Mu tumaku gotia bahi dheithili.' A syntactic possibility in one language does not have equivalence in another language. I am inclined to agree with K.V. Tirumalesh who gave the following example in this context:

> As another example, consider the story of Narcissus narrated by Robert Graves in his excellently written book *Greek Myths*. Narcissus is so handsome that whoever looks at him falls in love with him at first sight. But he is also vain and so spurns all offers of love. One day he goes stag-hunting along with his friends. Echo is one of the several young women in love with him and secretly follows him wherever he goes. On that particular day Narcissus gets separated from his companions in the forest. Realizing that he has strayed, he calls: "Is anyone here?" Echo hears him and is only too anxious to respond. But then she is under a terrible curse from Hera. Echo can only repeat what the others may say: she can never say anything new on her own. So the 'conversation' between Narcissus and Echo goes along the following lines:
>
> "Is anyone here?"
>
> "Here!"
>
> "Come!"
>
> "Come!"
>
> "Why do you avoid me?"
>
> "Why do you avoid me?"
>
> "Let us come together here!"
>
> "Let us come together here!"

And so Echo gladly rushes from her hiding place to embrace Narcissus. But he rudely shakes her off and says: "I will die before you ever lie with me!" Seizing this wonderful opportunity of making her point, Echo repeats the last part of the sentence and pleads: "Lie with me!" The rest of the story is well-known: Echo was never able to win the love of Narcissus and was ultimately reduced to a feeble voice. The important thing about this example is the ingenuity with which Robert Graves has narrated the story. Since Echo can only repeat what the other person has said, she has to wait for the most opportune moment to make her point. And this is exactly what the storyteller has provided for in the last sentence of the dialogue. The words 'lie with me' exactly summarise what Echo really wants to say to Narcissus. Notice that this is a syntactic possibility that the English language permits. Suppose that you want to translate this into Kannada or any other language in which the subordinate clauses occur on the left of the main clause. Echo then will not be able to make her point in this way since she can only repeat either the whole utterance or the last part of it. She has no other choice. Right-branching and left-branching become crucial syntactic differences in such situations.[3]

The ontological and structural considerations point towards the limits of translation. The translator should not only possess an inwardness with both the languages—the SL and the TL, but he should know his subject well. In case of translation of metafiction which is atleast as much about itself as it is 'about' anything else at all, the translator has to be able to understand and interpret this particular type of fiction and its internal resonances. In course of an article K. Balasubramanian and D.R. Mohan Raj underline the limits of translation.

"We must realize, however, the translation is a communication medium, with its own areas of usefulness and its own limitations. The language used in translation, especially of some types of fiction, hardly functions as language *per se*. We are all familiar with discussions regarding the autonomy available to a translator, the dynamism of a translation, its relationship to the original in its time-bound relevance (diachronic and synchronic translations of equal value), and so on. Irrespective of the ultimate worth of a translation, it should be recognized that the translator is completely limited in his use of the medium that was available for use in its fullest potential to the author of the original. Not only is creative instinct that gave the original impetus difficult to match in a translation, the translator's task is further complicated by the host of limitations imposed on him by both subject and audience."[4]

Culture-specific words are ethnic, historical and sociological in nature. They restrict the scope of translation and point towards the limits of translation. The pop-slang language used in some fiction is almost untranslatable. Rustic words and slangs, used in fiction enhance the limits of translation. How can one translate the slangs uttered by people belonging to the lower strata of the society in contemporary fiction? How does one translate the sound and rhythm of poetry into another language vastly different from the source language and its culture? How does one translate advertisements from one language into another? The limits of translation will stare in our face when we take up technical subjects and literature for translation into a language which is very much unlike the SL.

Translation of advertisements severely curtail the freedom of translators. Advertisements are concerned with style and therefore, they limit the scope of translatability. Analysis of the language of advertisements reveals that the language-patterns used for accomplishing the advertisers, is fairly limited in its selection and therefore, the scope of deviation is very limited. TV advertisements done in English when translated literally into regional languages have jarring effects on the ears. The translator has to maintain readability, and listening ability, memorability and selling ability in the target language. But this cannot be done easily. Translation of advertisements shows the limits of translatability.

To conclude, I should say that there are limits exceeding which in one direction translation ceases to be translation and exceeding another it becomes mere imitation. In other words, translation done within the limits of translating an original writing becomes successful. The best translation is that which though based on an original writing, never reads like a translation. It gives us the feel of an original writing done in the source language.

## NOTES

1. Theodore, Savory, *The Art of Translation* (London: Cape, 1957) 156.
2. *Ibid.*, 16.
3. K.V. Tirumalesh, "Translation as Literature Three," *The Literary Criterion* 15: 3 (1990): 4-5.
4. Kamakshi Balasubramanian and D.R. Mohan Raj, "Contextual Vs Textual Specifics: The Limits of Translation," *Literature in Translation.* Ed. Pramod Talgeri and S.B. Verma (Bombay: Popular Prakashan, 1988) 36.

# 9

# The Role of the Translator

Translation has been defined variously at different times in the past. For some, it is the falsifier of the original, for others, it is a carry over of meaning from source language (SL) to target language (TL) and still, for quite a few, it is a transference of meaning from SL to TL. All these definitions are partially true but inadequate to describe the meaning of translation in the full sense of the term. From these definitions we move away with the structuralists and the post-structuralists to describe translation variously as 'substitution of meaning,' 'regulated transformation,' 'after life' and finally, as 'cannibalism.' All the latest theorists have rejected the notion of original being primary and translation as secondary. There is no such dichotomy between the original and the translated text, for the original is itself a translation of ideas, notions and so on. If the notion of translation has changed over the years, what should be the role of a translator?

The translator like the critic has been traditionally considered as inferior to the creative writer. But now, thanks to the post-structuralists, the critic is taken as co-creator and criticism as co-creation. Can we envisage such a role for a translator?

What are the qualifications of a translator? He must know two languages—the source language (SL) and the target language (TL)—equally well. A creative writer or a critic can perform his role well by being monolingual but a translator must be a bilingual. Not only that, he must have inwardness with both the languages. Otherwise, he can't be a good translator.

In 1970s there was a move in U.S.A. to give due recognition to the translator. The translator deserves to be known along with the creative writer, for he like the latter moulds words and phrases and gives them 'a local habitation and a name.' Let us, examine the way the translator works. Here are a few options before him: one, if he renders word for word, he will be accused of being unimaginative and dull; two, if he takes liberty with the original and recreates it in the target language, he will be accused of infidelity, and lose his credibility. Whatever the translation theorists may say, the purpose of translation is to make the source language text available in the target language for the readers to get the true meaning of it. Reading is primarily meant for meaning (or sense), then comes the aesthetic enjoyment. To do his job successfully, the translator has to develop his linguistic skill and cultural insight into both the languages (SL and TL).

The translator of a literary text should be conversant not only with two languages but with two literatures. Here, comes the question of intertextuality. The meaning of a text is dependent on other texts that precedes it. One may go along with Jonathan Culler to say that every text is a mosaic of citations from other texts which it absorbs and transforms. For example, how can one fully understand—let alone appreciate—*The Waste Land* and *Four Quartets* without referring to the *Upanishadas* and the *Bhagavat Gita* for Eliot has made several allusions to these two Indian texts? The translator has to be a scholar and a critic to translate a literary text. Unless he is widely read and has deep insight into the nuances of literary text he can't successfully translate it. Moreover, each text has more than one meaning. The multiplicity of meaning and the indeterminacy of such meanings in a literary text according to post-structuralists make the task of the translator all the more difficult. From the linguistic point of view for each word in a language there is no corresponding word in another language—that is, there is no equivalence of words in two languages. Hence, word for word translation will be a self-defeating exercise. What is more acceptable is sense for sense translation. When that kind of exercise fails, the translator may take recourse to transliteration. So translator has to keep these three terms—translation, transcreation and transliteration—in mind while undertaking the task of translation.

A translator can perform in two ways—one, he may translate from the second language or foreign language into the first language (let us say, mother tongue) and in this case, the second language or foreign language becomes the source language and mother tongue becomes the target language and two, he may translate from the mother tongue into the foreign language and in this case the mother tongue becomes the source language and foreign language becomes the target language. Migrant and diasporic writers do a lot of translation to resituate themselves in their past and country. As Stephanos Stephanides has rightly put it:

> Translation theory normally assumes that the translator translates into the mother tongue from the foreign language. The self is the target or home culture and the source is the other or foreign culture; however, this easy binary becomes problematic with the migrant translator moving between systems (35).

The insights into 'home' and 'foreign' comes through translation. It is not true to say that something is always lost in translation and instead, we can say that something is also gained in it. Let me take a long quotation from Stephanides to explain this point: "In his essay *Imaginary Homelands*, Rushdie begins by citing the opening sentence of L.P. Hartley's *The Go-Between*: "The past is a foreign country, they do things differently there" but as he looks at a photograph on the wall of his house in Bombay taken in 1946, he suggests that the idea should be inverted making the present foreign and "past is home, albeit a lost home in a lost city in the mists of lost time" (9). He then describes a return visit to his house in Bombay after an absence of more than half his life, and states in terms recalling Walter Benjamin's. "Thesis on the Philosophy of History" (in *Illuminations* 254) that in an eerie kind of way the past claimed him, and the facts of his faraway life became illusions: "the colours of my history had seeped out of my mind's eye; now my other two eyes were assaulted by colours." This experience he says was when his novel *Midnight's Children* was really born, as he tried to restore the past to himself through "shards of memory like the broken pots of antiquity, from which the past can sometimes, but always provisionally, be reconstructed, are exciting to discover, even if they are pieces of the most quotidian objects" (12). While conceding that the past is a country from which we have all migrated, the experience of this loss is intensified in the migrant who is distant in space as well as time, out-of-country and ever out-of-language. From his inversion of the idea that the past is a foreign country to the idea that the past is home, Rushdie extends the notion of geographical migration to translations and thus reverse the usual paradigm of the translation tradition where the target language is self (or the domestic tradition) and the source is the other. Though he begins with an inversion of the notions of the home and the foreign, self and other, the binary collapses and the diasporic subject becomes a hybrid existing or encoded in modes of translation, such that the postcolonial writer inscribes the (m)other tongue into English. In his essay "Errata" (in *Imaginary Homelands* 1991: 24), he explains deliberate errors of fact in his personal redefinition of Indian history in *Midnight's Children* and says his subject had changed, it "was no longer a search for lost time, it had become the way in which we remake the past to suit our present purposes, using memory as our tool." Though the migrant loses language and home he is not simply transformed by his act; he also transforms his new world and it is through this hybridization that newness can emerge. Rushdie returns repeatedly to the idea of the translated man in his fiction, in his insistence on exploring how newness comes into the world and that his is not simply a subject lost in translation (35-37).

Translations are subjected to at least two different semiotic systems—that is, source and target languages. Walter Benjamin in his essay, "The Task of the Translator" explained this double constitution quite well. Translation is viewed as a 'mode' of its own, on which offers a way of "coming to terms with the foreignness of languages" (W. Benjamin, trans. Zohn 75).

Translators should have linguistic competence in both the languages—the source language and the target language—to do their job well. Apart from that they should have literary competence to undertake the task of translation. It is not always easy to do a faithful translation of a literary text written in a language which is vastly different from the target language and target culture. For example, English is S.V.O. language (subject followed by verb and object in that order) while most of the Indian languages including Oriya are S.O.V. languages (subject followed by object and verb in that order) and to do a faithful translation of an English literary text into any of the Indian languages is not an easy task. There are numerous socio-cultural terms in our languages which cannot be rendered into English. In that case the translator should take recourse to transliteration and give a footnote to explain the terms. For example, 'Ekoisa' (21st day celebrations) of a child is performed in Hindu Houses in Orissa which has no equivalent in English. So the translator may render it into English by saying "naming ceremony" which falls on the 21st day of a child's birth. Similarly many food items, dresses, elements connected with rituals in our society should be rendered into English through transliteration.

Jokes, colloquial words, slangs can be rendered into another language through transliteration and free translation. The translator should take note of all these difficulties while translating literary texts into the target language. Take for example, "Kanale Kuha" in Oriya which has a touch of irony about it. To translate this word into English as 'soft-spoken' will be self-defeating for the English word is used in a positive sense. Instead of 'soft-spoken' if we translate it as "Sweet-Talker" the irony can be brought home. Sometimes the translator has to transcreate words instead of merely translating them in an inauthentic way. Transcreation is done with insight both by the translator and the self-translator.

Self-translators are those who translate their own work into the target language. Rabindranath Tagore, Samuel Beckett, Girish Karnad and Manoj Das belong to this category. Tagore and Beckett are the two authors so far to win Nobel Prize for Literature for translated works. This is because, they have transcreated their own work into English—Tagore translated from Bengali (his mother tongue) into English, whereas Beckett translated from French into English (his mother tongue). Girish Karnad first writes his plays in Kannada and then translates (rather, transcreates) them into English, and that is why, he is taken to be an Indian English dramatist. Vijay Tendulkar writes in Marathi and his plays too are translated into English (by others, not by himself) and that is why he is not regarded as an Indian English dramatist. Manoj Das sometimes writes his stories first in Oriya (his mother tongue) and then writes these stories in English taking liberty with them because he transcreates them into English. Translators don't enjoy the privilege of the self-translators because they are not the authors of the texts which they translate into the target language. Sometimes authors express their dissatisfaction with the translation of their works and blame the translators for it. But self-translators don't complain because they are the authors of the both original and translated texts.

There is a universal problem about translation which every translator faces. That is, should a translator translate what the author says or what he means? Some say, it is not the business of the translator to say what the author means because that is the job of the critic. Other say that the translator should endeavour to say what the author says and leave it to the readers to read meanings into it. But this seems to be not a correct approach. The translator should say both—what the author says and what he means. Otherwise, translation would lose its importance and the translator, his credibility.

In the post-structuralist parlance the argument goes like this: that is, each text is like a palimpsest and it is the indeterminacy of meaning that makes the text open-ended. Interpretation of a literary text is never ending. In that case, what should a translator do? Which meaning he is going to translate into the target language? Since each text is a linguistic as well as cultural construct, the translator should possess linguistic ability and cultural inwardness in order to render a text into another language.

It is said that the translator is invisible—he merely ferries the text across languages. But this is not true. Just as the original text bears the interior signature of the author the translated text bears the interior signature of the translator. That is why no two translations of a particular text are similar and of equal merit. It depends on the competence of the translator to make the translated text read like the original. Hence, translator is a performer and a creator.

Translator is not only a creator but a comparatist. As Comparative Literature depends on translation for its growth and development, it has become in the words of Bassnett and Lefevere, "a subcategory of Translation Studies" (12). And therefore, the translator has become a comparatist who knows two languages (SL and TL) and two literatures (original and translated) well. A translator is both a reader and a writer. He reads a text like a reader and writes it through his translation. He interprets the text as he reads it and re-creates it as he translates it.

To conclude, I should say that the translator has a significant role to play to make the literary text available in the target language. He promotes, though obliquely the cause of Comparative Literature in the present context. It would not be wrong to say that a translator combines in him the role of the three—writer, critic and comparatist—and makes translation look and read like the original. No wonder, we in India always take translation as 'new writing' and translator as creator.

## WORKS CITED

Bassnett, Susan and Andre Lefevere. Eds. *Translation, History and Culture*, London: Pinter, 1990.

Benjamin, Walter. *Illuminations*. Trans. Harry Zohn. New York: Schocken Books, 1969.

Stephanides, Stephanos. "Imagining the Homeland and in Translation." *The Literary Criterion* 38: 2 (2003).

# 10

# Translator's Dilemma: Agony or Ecstasy?*

> In the beginning was the word, and the word was translation, and with it God translated the human and the earth. But the earth was without form and void, and darkness was upon the face of the deep, and the word moved upon the face of the waters, translating the light from the darkness.
>
> —Pierre Grange

A creative writer may be monolingual, a critic may be unilingual but a translator happens to be a bilingual. A translator could be a polyglot, a linguist but he should also have the insight of a critic. The job of a translator is to render an already existing text into another language. A creative writer or a critic has no such problem. While translator does the job of a creative writer and in the process he also undertakes the job of a critic in trying to get the meanings inherent in the source language text. Whatever the translation theorists may say, the translator not merely says what the creative writer says in SL text but he also writes what the creative writer means. That means, the TL text should not only say what the SL text says but mean as well. Therein comes the dilemma of a translator. In course of this lecture, I will explain the task of the translator by taking into consideration the nature, scope and theory of translation.

In his essay titled, "The Task of the Translator" in 1939 Walter Benjamin, "Wrote of translation as a mode that depends

---

* This chapter was delivered as a Plenary Lecture at National seminar on "Translations as Rebirth: Revisiting Canonical Indian Literature in English Translation" organised by the Researchers' Association, Odisha on 26-27 May 2012.

upon the translatability of a work—can anyone translate it? Does a work lend itself to the act of translation and thereby call for it" (Selby 128).

Benjamin's statement makes it clear that though some works yield to translation all works are not translatable. Should we lay our hands off and point out that this and this work are untranslatable. That is the translator's dilemma. Before analyzing this problem let us have a bird's eye view of origin and growth of translation both in the west and in the east. It is presumed that in the beginning mankind was speaking only one language, as the birds of the species do. But when the Babylonians were building the Tower of Babel, they were utterly confused and one didn't understand what the other one was speaking of. Hence, there was the loss of the common language of man, which led to the birth of translation. Translation, in the west owes its origin to the second fall of man—that is, the loss of a common language. The origin of translation in India is untraceable. Sujit Mukherjee puts it persuasively in the following passage:

> Our ancients may not have invented translation—they didn't even seem to have coined a term for it—but there is ample evidence of a literary text passing from one language into another. The most re-assuring example of this from the very early pre-colonial times is that of *Brihatkatha* of Gunadhya, who composed this voluminous cycle of stories in prose in the 4th or 5th century A.D. in a Prakrit speech somewhat dismissively named as Paisachi. The original text is lost but versions were preserved in other languages—three Sanskrit texts, two Prakrit abridgements, and one Tamil fragment. An even older example would be that of the Jataka tales, each telling of a former birth of the Buddha, first collected in Pali and forming the tenth book of *Khaddanikaya.* These stories were later developed in Sanskrit, mixing prose and verse, as full-fledged narratives. Neither of these two examples is of translation in the modern sense of the term, but they both embody the choice as well as compulsion which required texts to be reborn in another language. The practice of translation surely relates to such choices and compulsions (22).

Translator unlike the original creative writer does not only write the text but reads the SL text before hand. Hence, translation is two-in-one activity—i.e. reading and writing. It is reader centred (i.e. translator is a reader first, only after that a writer). If texts could be 'readerly' as well as 'writerly' (courtesy, Roland Barthes), intersexuality an accepted norm (courtesy, Julia Kristeva), then which meaning a translator should take while rendering SL text into TL text? This adds to the translator's dilemma.

Theories of translation make the task of the translator all the more complicated. Translation has been variously described as 'an art' (Theodore Savory's Coinage), 'a craft' (Eric Jacobsen's definition) and 'a science' (Eugene Nida's description) and interpreted as 'carry over of meaning', 'substitution of meaning', 'transference of meaning' between two languages (source language and target language). All these observations are correct in their contexts. But theories of translation which though developed through different centuries, got their legitimacy when Paul Engle, Director of Writers' Workshop at the University of Iowa organized a translation workshop in 1964 by hiring a full time director for it.

The earlier notions like 'translation is inferior to the original', infidel to the original came under fire with polysystem theorists like Evan Itamar Zohar and Gideon Toury and feminist theorists like Lori Chamberlain, Susan Bassnett, Barbara Johnson and others challenging the traditional concepts as untrue. Deconstructionist went a step further by stating that the original is a work of translation (bears echoes of the quotation cited as 'epigraph' taken from Majumdar's article) and translation as 'regulated transformation'. Thus, translation moved away from the notion of structuralism as 'a linguistic activity' to post-structuralism and became a cultural activity. We moved away from Tel Aviv Group to Canadian Feminist translation theorists and then to the Brazilian Cannibalist theorists like .Haroldo and Augusto de Campos. Cannibalistic theory of translation is in line with polysystem theory, feminist translation theory and deconstructionist theory in rejecting the power structure that privileges the original text over the translated text. As Susan Bassnett puts it:

> The images of translation as Cannibalism, as Vampirism whereby the translator sucks out the blood of the source text to strengthen the target text, as transfusion of blood that endows the receiver with new life, can all be seen as radical metaphors that spring from postmodernist postcolonial translation theory (155).

We in India have been translating from Sanskrit into other bhashas thousands years ago. G.N. Devy rightly observes:

> Most modern Indian languages initiated their respective literary traditions with translations of works from Sanskrit, either the epics—*Ramayana* and *Mahabharata*—or philosophical texts like the *Gita*. During the first four centuries of their existence—thirteenth to the sixteenth centuries—there were numerous translations from one regional language to another regional language, numerous instances of literary bilingualism as well as many important translations from Indian languages to Persian and Arabic, the two languages of political domination during these centuries. The contemporary scene in the field of literary translation in India shows a comparable vitality of translation interest; and the similarity between the two translation epochs should be of interest; and the similarity and literary theories (117-18).

What baffles us is this: that is inspite of a long tradition of translation in our country, "Why isn't there a single critical text specifying the art or science of translation parallel to Panini's *Ashtdhyayi* or Tolkapier's *Tolkapium* or Bharata's *Natyashastra*" (Choudhuri 113).

Translation became political during the colonial period. The west being scared of the 'other' oriental culture entering their lives through translation, started translating from India. Warren Hastings, the Governor General of Bengal (1772-85) is believed to have encouraged the translation of *Dharmasastras* from 'Sanskrit into Persian by Indians and then from Persian into English by Europeans' (Mukherjee 34). Charles Wilkins translated the *Bhagavad Gita* into English in 1774 published by the Asiatic Society of Bengal in Calcutta and William Jones had translated.

Kalidasa's *Sakuntala and the Ring of Recollection* (5th c.) in 1789 and *The Laws of Manu 1* (2nd BCE - 2nd c. CE) in 1779. R. Parthasarathy makes a very pertinent comment on the politics behind such translations:

> We must not allow ourselves to forget that politics was the moving force behind these earliest translations of Sanskrit texts in the eighteenth century. Warren Hastings (1732-1818), the governor-general of Bengal, encouraged Wilkins and Jones in their translations, since a first-hand knowledge of Indian traditions would be invaluable in governing India. The relationship between England and India was a relationship of power and domination. Translation was an instrument of police that helped in orientalizing India so that it became a province of European thought. It is therefore not surprising that Indian literature in English translation has usually been read in terms of Western poetics, an inappropriate approach originating in the political aims of *pax Britannica.* I consider the Eurocentric view of Indian literature as essentially hegemonic (*IL* 170).

In the postcolonial era many bhasha writers in their effort to reach a wider audience and to compete the Indian English writers in terms of national and international visibility allowed their works to be translated into English. The British taught us their language and our profit on it is that we learnt how to translate our work into their language (apart from writing directly in English). A.K. Ramanujan a great poet and a greater translator, who made U.R. Annathamurthy's *Samskara* famous by translating it into English, makes the point clear in course of an interview to A.L. Becker and Keith Taylor. He says,

> English has distorted our traditions, but it has also made us look at our traditions. It's not enough to say that it is all colonialism and has done nothing but distort. This whole question of colonial distortion has been formulated in English. It requires a dialogue with English. English has been the "other" through which we have returned to ourselves (79).

Both Parthasarathy and Ramanujan are right in their assessment of the context in which translation is used in our country. In a way Parthasarathy illustrates Ramanujan's point when he says,

> The discovery of European scholars of Panini's Sanskrit grammar, "The Eight Chapters" or the *Ashtadhyayi,* usually dated 4th c. BCE, revolutionized the science of linguistics in the nineteenth century. No European language, not even Greek and Latin, had previously been described with such scientific exactitude (*IL* 171).

Hence, translation becomes discovery for 'others' and recovery for 'us.' No wonder, Sujit Mukherjee a well-known scholar has titled two of his books on translation as *Translation as Discovery and Other Essays* (1981) and *Translation as Recovery* (2009).

A question that disturbs me is that why should the Westerners be the law-givers—be it literary theory or translation theory—and we are left just to study what they do? Indian academics in the universities and outside merely recycle western theories endlessly and not tired of repeating them, when most of them can be contested, refuted and rejected when viewed from Indian stand-point. Keeping this in mind let us turn to translation and the task of the translator in our situation.

The opening sentence of Vinay Dharwadker's essay, "Translating the Millennium: Indian Literature in the Global Market" makes the stand of translation clear our context. The sentence runs as follows:

> In its basic sense, translation—*anuvad* in Sanskrit, Hindi, Marathi and other Indian languages, and *tarjuma* in Arabic, Parsi and Urdu—is the representation of a text in one language with a parallel verbal composition to another language (*IL* 133).

In Odiya translation is 'anuvad'. He is of the opinion that basic Indian terms for translation, *bhashantara, rupantara* and *anukarana* corresponds to John Dryden's three types of translation, 'metaphase', 'paraphrase' and 'imitation' (*IL* 136-37). What creates problems for the Indian translator is the structure of languages. For each word in a language there is not a corresponding word in another language. Most of the Indian languages are SOV (subject, object followed by verb) languages, when English is a SVO (subject, verb followed by object) language. Hence word order can't be maintained in translating from Indian bhashas into English and *vice versa*. Hence, as A.K. Ramanujan has suggested that, "the best strategy is to render the text, 'phrase by phrase', 'step-wise,' structural unit by structural unit" (*The Interior Landscape* 11-12). Hence, "the relation between translation and original is not equivalence but parallelism," (*IL* 137) says Dharwadker.

The second major problem of the translator is to dive deep into the deep structure of the original text for meaning is not inherent in the language of the text but in the literary tradition and culture to which the text belongs. The deep structure explains the inner meaning of the text. Here comes the Indian critical tradition to our rescue. According to Dharwadker, "this 'inner logic' is buried not only in the original language but also in its literary tradition and ambient culture, it is part of what we call *bhavartha* (implied meaning), *dhvani* (the resonance of suggestions), and *sandarbha* (context)" (*IL* 139).

Since the translation is primarily meant for a reader who does not know the original language, the translator's problem is not only to translate the text into the reader's language but to make the reader see into the literary tradition and culture of the original language. This is a Herculean task, which adds to the agony of the translator.

Another problem of the translator is to translate jokes proverbs, culture specific words, food items, dress materials, etc. from one language into another. Here, he has to take recourse to transliteration, while translating poems in general and ancient poems in particular the translator faces a dilemma. That is, the translation should be a poem—not a prose paraphrase. Denotative meaning, connotative meaning, intertextuality—all these are to be taken into account. 'The poetic sensibility ought to be preserved. That's the agony.

Let us take the other side of the translator's task. We know that one original text can have several translated/transcreated texts (should we say texts generate other texts?). The best example is the different versions of the *Ramayana* and the *Mahabharata* in bhasha literatures. Would it not be correct to say that translation is generative transformation? If the original text is generated in another language through translation, keeping the 'essence' (say 'atma') intact, then to an Indian mind translation becomes rebirth. Again as R. Parthasarathy say, "the translator unearths long forgotten classics and puts them into orbit, thus redrawing the literary map" (*IL* 170).

To conclude, I should say that translation is partly creative and partly critical, because it combines the translator's critical acumen and creative insight. It's not only an act of journey between two languages but an interconnective activity between creation and criticism. The translator is a builder who builds a new text carved out of the original. The original and the translation become two sides of the same coin at the hands of a good translator, not quite the same but inseparable. That's the ecstasy of the translator.

## WORKS CITED

Bassnett, Susan. *Comparative Literature: A Critical Introduction.* Oxford: Blackwell Publishers Ltd., 1998. Print.

Becker, A.L. and Keith Taylor. "Interview Two". A.K. Ramanujan, *Uncollected Poems and Prose.* Eds. Molly Daniels—Ramanujan and Keith Harrison. New Delhi: OUP, 2011. Print.

Choudhuri, Indra Nath. "Towards and Indian Theory of Translation". *Indian Literature.* 54:5 (Sept/Oct. 2010): 113-23.

Devy, G.N. *In Another Tongue: Essays on Indian Literature in English.* Madras: MacMillan India Ltd., 1995. Print.

Dharwadker, Vinay. "Translating the Milennium: Indian Literature in the Global Market." *Indian Literature* 52:4 (July/Aug. 2008): 133-46. Print.

Majumdar, Keya. "Appropriating the 'Others': Some Challenges of Translation and its Theories". *Indian Literature.* 50:4 (July/Aug. 2006): 163-70. Print.

Mukherjee, Sujit. *Translation as Recovery.* Ed. Meenakshi Mukherjee. Delhi: Pencraft International, 2009. Print.

Ramanujan, A.K. *The Interior Landscape: Love Poems from a Classical Tamil Anthology.* Bloomington, Indiana: Indiana University Press, 1967.

Selby, Martha Ann. "On the Translatability of Intention in Indian Poetry," *Indian Literture* 32:1 (Jan/Feb. 1989): 128: 140.

# 11

# A Critique of Translation Theories

Translation is a form of communication between two languages—the source language and the target language. At the spoken level it is an interpretation of the source language for the hearer in the target language. But at the writing level, translation is always considered as rewriting of the original text. In other words translation is a text about a text and hence, it is a meta-text. It reproduces not only what the author in the original language [*i.e.* the source language (SL)] says but what he means. It has been variously described: as 'an art,' (Theodore Savory's term) as 'a craft' (Eric Jacobsen's term) and as a 'Science' (Eugene Nida's coinage) but none of these terms is fully adequate. 'Art' is creative and an expression of beauty, while 'craft' has a 'lower status occupation' of amateurishness and trickery. The opinion about translation as a purely mechanistic process springs from an obsession with science. In fact, translation is more than all these—'art,' 'craft,' and 'science.' It is a process of analysis, interpretation and creation which leads to a replacement of one set of linguistic resources and values for another.

"Translation Theory" is and is not a new field; though it has existed only since 1983 as a separate entry in the Modern Language Association International Bibliography, it is as old as the tower of Babel (Gentzler 1993: 1). Before analysing the Contemporary Translation Theories, we would do well to take a bird's eye view of what we call the status of Translation in the preceding centuries in order to put the subject in its proper perspective.

The credit of formulating a systematic theory of Translation goes to the French humanist Etienne Dolet who published a short outline of the principles of translation titled, La maniere de bien traduire d'une langue en aultre (How to Translate well from one Language into Another) in 1540. Dolet laid down five cardinal principles for the translator:

(1) The translator must fully understand the sense and meaning of the original author, although he is at liberty to clarify obscurities.

(2) The translator should have a perfect knowledge of both SL and TL.

(3) The translator should avoid word-for-word renderings.

(4) The translator should use forms of speech in common use.

(5) The translator should choose and order words appropriately to produce the correct tone.

Dolet's principles, ranked as they are in a precise order, stress the importance of understanding the SL text as a primary requisite. The translator is far more than a competent linguist, and translation involves both a scholarly and sensitive appraisal of the SL text and an awareness of the place the translation is intended to occupy in the TL system (Bassnett-McGuire 1991: 54).

George Chapman, the great translator of Homer in his dedication of the *Seven Books* (1598) echoed Dolet's views of translation, in his prescription for the translator to avoid word for word translation and to make an attempt to catch the spirit of the original. The act of translation during the Renaissance aimed at nativising European languages and that is why, *The Bible* and the works of Homer received the attention of the translators. But it was John Dryden, who in his preface to *Ovid's Epistles* (1680) underlined the three basic types of translation:

> (i) Metaphase, or turning an author word by word and line by line, from one language into another; (ii) paraphrase, or translation with latitude, the Ciceronian 'sense-for-sense' view of translation; (iii) imitation, where the translator can abandon the text of the original as he sees fit. (Bassnett-McGuire 60)

In the eighteenth century, to be precise in 1791 Alexander Fraser Tytler published a book titled *The Principles of Translation*, which is, in the opinion of Susan Bassnett-McGuire 'the first systematic study in English of the translation processes.' Tytler outlines three basic principles:

> (i) The translation should give a complete transcript of the idea of the original work; (ii) the style and manner of writing should be of the same character with that of the original; (iii) the translation should have all the ease of the original composition. (Bassnett-McGuire 63)

In the Romantic age there are two attitudes to translation—one view holds that it is a category of thought and hence, creative in nature, and the other view holds that translation is a mechanical process of making known a text in another language. G.N. Devy makes an interesting observation when he says that, "while the Renaissance translations were attempts to raise the status of the translators' culture, the Romantic translations were aimed at raising the cultural status of the works translated. Their minimum requirement was to seem exotic without being essentially unEnglish or unGerman" (1993: 137).

In the Post-Romantic period translators like Friedrich Schleiermacher, F.W. Newman, Carlyle and William Morris pleaded for a separate sub-language for translation (*i.e.* translation language) and wanted the translator to retain the peculiarity of the original wherever possible. Matthew Arnold laid emphasis on the SL Text and wanted that the translation to be committed to it (*i.e.*, a close fidelity to the SL Text). In his first lecture on *Translating Homer*, Arnold says:

> Let not the translator, then, trust to his notions of what the ancient Greeks would have thought of him; he will lose himself in the vague. Let him not trust to what the ordinary English reader thinks of him; he will be taking the blind for his guide. Let him not trust to his own judgement of his own work; he may be misled by individual caprices. Let him ask how his work affects those who both know Greek and can appreciate poetry. (1914: 247)

Literal translation has been emphasized by other translators as well. Henry Wadsworth Longfellow speaking of his translation of Dante's *Divina Commedia* underlines that:

> The business of a translator is to report what the author says, not to explain what he means; that is the work of the commentator. What an author says and how he says it, that is the problem of the translator. (Desua 1964: 65)

On the other hand, it was Edward Fitzgerald, well-known for his translation of *The Rubaiyat of Omar Khayyam* (1858) who pleaded for taking liberty with the original text and creating a new TL text. He made the "famous remark that it were better to have a live sparrow than a stuffed eagle," (Bassnett-McGuire 1991: 70-71). Translation has to be exotic. This point has been emphasized by Frank Kermode when he praised *Omar's Rubayats* in Fitzgerald's translation:

> Where Omar asks for a loaf, a jug of wine, a sheep's thigh and a pretty boy, Fitzgerald omits the meat, substitutes a 'Thou,' and introduces a poetry book (which no Persian scholar would need) and a Bough, which is not a property of Persian wilderness. When we see that the translator's first prose shot said "a bit of mutton and moderate bottle of wine," we become aware that, having left Persian poetry out, Fitzgerald was putting English poetry in, and his changes obscurely touch the heart of a people which rarely reads verses and, rarely drinks wine. He is exotic without being foreign. (1968: 61)

Translation is a scholarly activity and the translator has to be instinctively bilingual. He must have an inwardness with both the languages (*i.e.*, the SL and the TL), while some translators have advocated close fidelity to the text and emphasized literal translation, others have pleaded for taking some liberty with the S.L. text and creating a new TL text. This was the nature of debate on the art of translation from the earlier times to the First World War. I am inclined to agree with Susan Bassnett-McGuire's view on this point expressed in the following words:

> The main currents of translation typology in a great age of industrial capitalism and colonial expansion up to the First World War can loosely be classified as follows:

> (1) Translation as a scholar's activity, where the pre-eminence of the SL text is assumed *de facto* over any TL version.
>
> (2) Translation as a means of encouraging the intelligent reader to return to the SL original.
>
> (3) Translation as a means of helping the TL reader become the equal of what Schleiermacher called the better reader of the original, through a deliberately contrived foreignness in the TL text.
>
> (4) Translation as a means whereby the individual translator who sees himself like Aladdin in the enchanted vaults (Rossetti's imaginative image) offers his own pragmatic choice to the TL reader.
>
> (5) Translation as a means through which the translator seeks to upgrade the status of the SL text because it is perceived as being on a lower cultural level.
>
> From these five categories, it can be seen that types (1) and (2) would tend to produce very literal, perhaps pedantic translations, accessible to a learned minority, whilst types (4) and (5) could lead to much freer translations that might alter the SL text completely in the individual translator's eclectic process of treating the original. The third category, perhaps the most interesting and typical of all, would tend to produce translations full of archaisms of form and language, and it is this method that was so strongly attacked by Arnold when he coined the verb to *newmanize*, after F.W. Newman, a leading exponent of this type of translation. (1991: 71-72)

Modern translation theory like modern critical theory begins with the advent of structuralism and gets proliferated in the recent years (*i.e.* in the last four decades of the twentieth century). It has developed from the linguistic approach of the nineteen sixties through the textual focus of the seventies to the culturally based approach of the eighties and after. It may be mentioned here that the history of translation theory until Roman Jakobson as a continual reiteration of the same formal (basing upon the form of the original writing) versus free (taking a liberty with the form of the original to make it innovative) theoretical distinction. "Over some two thousand years of argument and precept, the beliefs and disagreements voiced about the nature of translation have been almost the same," says George Steiner and further adds, "Identical theses, familiar moves and refutations in debate recur, nearly without exception, from Cicero and Quintilian to the present day" (1975: 239). Tejaswini Niranjana almost echoes the sentiment of Steiner when she says:

> Western writings on translation go back at least to the beginning of Judeo-Christian time. There never seems, however, to have been much of an attempt to formulate a discipline or an institutional apparatus to regulate translators. Only in the present century (*i.e.* the 20th century)—coinciding with but largely unmarked by, the rise of post-structuralism in literary studies—have there been efforts to give an institutional character to translation through the publication of journals devoted to translation and the formation of professional organizations. (1990: 49-50)

Edwin Gentzler underlines five different approaches to translation beginning with mid-sixties till date:

> (1) American translation workshop, (2) the 'science' of translation, (3) early translation studies, (4) polysystem theory and translation studies, and (5) deconstruction. (1993: 2)

Till 1963 there was no translation centers, no association of literary translation, no journal exclusively devoted to translation studies in U.S.A. Paul Engle, Director of Writers' Workshop at the University of Iowa, hired a full time director for the first translation workshop in 1964 and gave, as it were, 'a local habitation and a name' to translation studies by recognising the academic merit of literary translations. In 1965 "the Ford Foundation conferred a $150,000 grant on the University of Texas at Austin toward the establishment of the National Translation Center. Also in 1965, the first issue of *Modern Poetry in Translation*, edited by Ted Hughes and Daniel Weissbort, was published, providing literary translators a place for their creative work. In 1968, the National Translation Center published the first issue of *Delos*, a journal devoted to the history as well as the aesthetics of translation. Literary translation had established a place, albeit a small one, in the production of American culture" (Gentzler 8).

The process of acceptance of translation studies as a discipline was accelerated in the seventies with the introduction of translation courses and organization of translation workshops at several universities like Binghamton, Columbia, Iowa, Princeton, State University of New York, Texas and Yale, etc. in U.S.A. This growth of translation studies led to be establishment of the professional organization called American Literary Translators Association (ALTA) in the late seventies and the founding of the journal called Translation for that Association. Soon the need for translation as a weapon to serve the cause of the society in the contemporary world was felt by the intellectuals, in no uncertain terms. Paul Engle underlined the urgency of translation in his Foreword to *Writing From the World II* (1985) in the following words:

> As this world shrinks together like an ageing orange and all peoples in all cultures move closer together (however reluctantly and suspiciously) it may be that the crucial sentence for our remaining years on earth may be very simply:
>
> TRANSLATE OR DIE.
>
> The lives of every creature on the earth may one day depend on the instant and accurate translation of one word. (Engle and Engle 1985: 2)

I.A. Richards expounded his theory of translation in a paper titled, "Toward a Theory of Translating" (1953), which discussed how to compare translations to original texts. Richards feels that if translators agree on their purpose, it would not be difficult to evolve the appropriate methodology. He argued that 'the translator should not only be aware that a sign (I) indicates something; but that it also; (II) characterizes (says the same thing or something new about things); (III) realizes (presents with varying degrees of vividness); (IV) values; (V) influences (desires change); (VI) connects; and (VII) purposes (attempts to persuade) (Richards 1953: 252-53). Swearing, as an example of his component IV, places value on something in addition to indicating something. Thus "meaning" for Richards had grown to be something very complex, having both implicit and explicit aspects (Gentzler 1993: 16-17).

Seven years after Richards' paper, Quine in *Word and Object* (1960) wanted to use translation to demonstrate the inherent complexity and lack of determined meanings in language. In the preface to the book he says, "Language is a social art. In acquiring it we have to depend entirely on inter-subjectivity available cues as to what to say and when. Hence there is no justification for collating linguistic meanings" (1960: 9). In the chapter "Translation and Meaning" he outlines the nature of language which determines the process of translation. He writes:

> Manuals for translating one language into another can be set up in divergent ways, all compatible with the totality of speech dispositions, yet incompatible with one another. In countless places they will diverge in giving, as their respective translations of a sentence of the one language, sentences of the other language which stand to each other in no plausible sort of equivalence however loose. (Quine, 1960: 27)

Richards reinforces this view when he says:

> Translation theory has not only to work for better mutual comprehension between users of diverse tongues; more central still in its purposing is a more complete viewing of itself and of the comprehending which it should serve. (1953: 261)

Ezra Pound's theory of translation underlines the precise use of words. He also lays emphasis on the rhythm, diction and word order. In his essay "How to Read" Pound outlines the ways in which, 'language is charged or energized.' The three important ways are 'melopoeia' (the musical property), 'phanopoeia' (the visual property) and 'logopoeia,' (a complex property) which includes both the 'direct meaning' and the 'play' of the word in the context. Frederic Will in his book, *The Knife in the Stone* uses translation as a testing ground for his theory of metaphysical concept. He writes:

> The inter-translatability of languages is the firmest testing ground, and demonstration ground, for the existence of a single ideal body of literature. If there is any meaning, to the

> idea of such a body, it will show itself through as effort to equate literature in one language with literature is another. (Will, 1973: 42)

Language seems to be the main factor in shaping the course and goal of translation. W.S. Merwin in the introduction to *Selected Translations*, 1968-1978 says:

> But if we take a single word of any language and try to find an exact equivalent in another...we have to admit it cannot be done. A single primary denotation may be shared; but the constellation of secondary meanings; the movement of rings of associations, the etymological echoes, the sound and its own levels of association, do not have an equivalent because they cannot.... Yet if we continue, we reach a point where some sequence of the first language conveys a dynamic unit, a rudiment of form. Some energy of the first language begins to be manifest, not only in single words but in the charge of their relationship. (1979: 8)

Theory of translation up to the sixties underlines that "in the process of translation that which manifests itself is less what the language says and more what it does, *i.e.* words take on an energy in their contextual, intertextual life (Gentlzer, 1993: 40).

The culmination of translation theories in the sixties is represented by such seminal works as Eugene Nida's *Message and Mission* (1960) and *Toward a Science of Translating* (1964), Noam Chomsky's *Aspects of the Theory of Syntax* (1965). In fact Nida can be taken as one of the most significant theorists of translation studies in the twentieth century. Edwin Gentzler is right in saying that Nida's book, *Toward a Science of Translating*, has become the 'Bible' not just for Bible translation, but for translation theory in general (1993: 44). Nida outlines his translation methodology as follows:

> It is both scientifically and practically more efficient (1) to reduce the source text to its structurally simplest and most semantically evident kernels, (2) to transfer the meaning from source language to receptor language on a structurally simple level, and (3) to generate the stylistically and

semantically equivalent expression in the receptor language. (Nida, 1964: 68)

We can outline his model of translation process as follows:

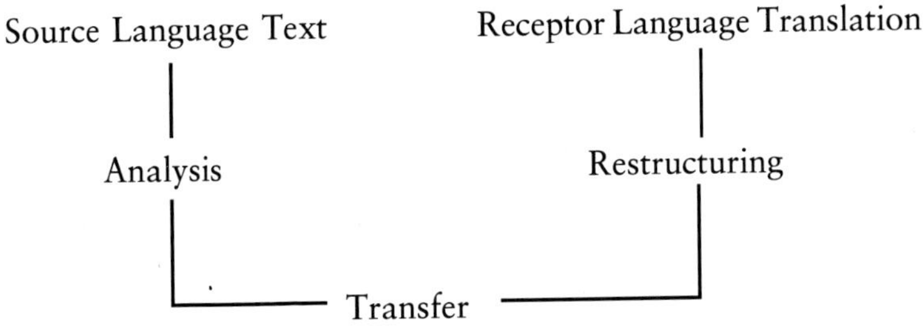


Translating for him is reproducing in the receptor language the closest natural equivalent of the message of the source language first in terms of meaning and second in terms of style.

If Nida's theory of translation draws upon Transformation Generative Grammar and Componential Semantics, J.C. Catford's theory of translation is based on M.A.K. Halliday's "Categories of theory of Grammar." His book, *A Linguistic Theory of Translation* is based on the theory of language and reminds us of Roman Jakobson's article titled "On Linguistic Aspects of Translation" in which the latter distinguishes three types of translation:

> (1) Intralingual translation or rewording (an interpretation of verbal sign by means of other signs in the same language). (2) Interlingual translation or translation proper (an interpretation of verbal signs by means of some other language). (3) Intersemiotic translation or transmutation (an interpretation of verbal signs by means of signs of non-verbal sign systems). (Brower 1959: 232)

Catford opines that any theory of translation must draw upon a theory of language—a general linguistic theory. He goes on to elaborate his theory by saying that translation is the replacement of textual material in the source language by an equivalent textual material in the target language. What happens in translation is not the transference of SL meanings into TL but a substitution TL meanings for SL meanings. Catford means to say that in the realms of translation substitution of meanings takes place but not transference of meanings. Translation equivalence occurs when the SL and TL texts are relatable to the features of substance. An SL text is translatable to a great degree though not absolutely. Untranslatability occurs when it becomes impossible to build functionally relevant features of the substitution into the contextual meaning of the TL text. Catford underlines two types of untranslatability which he terms linguistic and cultural. The central thesis of Catford's theory of translation is that it is neither a transference of meaning nor a transcoding of meaning but a substitution of meaning. Both Nida's theory and Catford's theory give a scientific basis to translation studies.

Speech Act Theory came into existence with the publication of J.L. Austin's William James lectures for 1955 under the title *How to Do Things with Words* and that gave rise to a Speech Act Theory of Translation. This theory of translation yields a topology based on the nature of the act—that is, the use of the language towards a specific end or its 'pragmatics.' Within this model the translator is taken both as an Addressor and an Addressee, R.D. Doctor illustrates this concept in the following way:

> Within the framework of a Speech Act Theory, at least two or more than two participants are involved which at least one is the Addressor and the other(s) is/are the addressee(s). The Addressor is the source of the message/code and hence also the source of the Illocutionary Act, since behind his utterance one can discern his intentions or his implications. The Addressee is the receiver of the message and hence is exposed to the perlocutionary value of the utterance. Curiously owing to the phenomenon of Communication Feedback the addressor also undergoes the perlocutionary effect: an often exploited comic situation is one in which a liar ends up himself a believing that his lies are truth, falling victim to his perlocutionary powers. The situation of the Translator is somewhat akin since the Translator is simultaneously Addressor and Addressee as the figure reveals:

| **Addressor 1A** | | **Addressee 1** | | **Addressor 1B** | | **Addressee 2** |
|---|---|---|---|---|---|---|
| Author/Text (Source-Text) | → | Translator as Reader | ↔ | Translator as Translator | → | Reader of Target-Text |

The Translator is an Addressee insofar as the Source-Text is concerned and an Addressor from the point of view of the Target-Text and its Reader/Addressee. But the resemblance is between the Translator and the Addressor, victim of his own perlocutionary skill rather than that of another addressor, the author. It cannot be denied that the Translator does have a Perlocutionary feedback but that is relatively less important than the perlocutionary impact of the Author/Text Addressee. It would hence be more correct within the framework of a Speech Act Theory to visualise the Translator as a Clearing-House for all three kinds of Speech Acts. This concept is not new: Mounin (1963) called the Translator a "Filter" through which the Source-Text was passed onto the Target-Text (Talgeri 1988; quoted in Das 1998: 87-88).

Important translation theorists of different countries of the world in the post-1970 period (*i.e.* from seventies to nineties) include James Holmes, Anton Popovic, Andre Lefevere, Gideon Toury, Jacques Derrida, Susan Bassnett-McGuire and Jose Lambert, who have given a new dimension to translation studies. Translator, Holmes draws our attention to the dual nature of translation in the following words:

> All translation is an act of critical interpretation, but there are some translations of poetry which differ from all other interpretative forms in that they also have an aim of being acts of poetry. It might be helpful if for this specific literary form with its double purpose as meta-literature and as primarily literature, we introduced the designation 'meta poem.' (1970: 93)

Andre Lefevere in his book, *Translating Poetry: Seven Strategies and a Blue Print* (1975) outlines the major task of the translator in the following words:

> The translator's task is precisely to render the source text, the original author's interpretation of a given theme expressed in a number of variations, accessible to readers not familiar

> with these variations, by replacing the original author's variations with their equivalents in a different language, time, place and tradition. Particular emphasis must be given to the fact that the translator has to replace all the variations contained in the source text by their equivalences. (1975: 99)

Gideon Toury in his *Translation Norms and Literary Translation* distinguishes among three kinds of translation norms: preliminary, initial and operational norms. Gentzler sums of Toury's views in the following words:

> Behind Early Translation Studies' definition of translation, argues Toury, is James Holmes' concept of "metatext," and although it has been elaborated by Anton Popovic (and others) and revised by Van den Broeck (and others), translated texts are still viewed by Translation Studies theorists as one kind of metatext, measured and evaluated in comparison with the source text or some idealised interpretation of that initial version (Toury 1980: 39). Toury wants to expand the boundaries of even that which early Translation Studies has already augmented, getting further away from hypothetical constructs that tend to study translated texts in isolation. As opposed to another Source Text (ST) determined theory, Toury posits a Target Text (TT) theory for translation, focusing not on some notion of equivalence as postulated requirements, but on the "actual relationships" constructed between the source text and its "factual replacement" (Toury, 1980: 39). He does not reject the work of contrastive linguistics or semiotic-functional approaches; linguistic/literary imitations of course operate and condition the nature of the translation product. He does argue, however, that such rules and laws are merely one set of factors operating on the translation process; his project introduces a new set of factors which may be more powerful than other factors. The eventual goal of Toury's theory is to establish a hierarchy of interrelated factors (constraints) which determine (govern) the translation product. In short, Toury demands that translation theory include cultural-historical "facts," a set of laws which he calls 'translation norms.' (Gentzler 1993: 129-30)

In the 1980s Translation Studies have acquired a new dimension. Translation is no longer viewed as a process of 'change into another language, retaining the sense' or 'substitution of SL textual material in TL,' 'a transference of meaning from SL to TL' but a 'regulated transformation' (Derrida's term). It is again defined as the 'migration through transformation of discursive elements (signs)' and as the 'process during which they are interpreted (re-contextualized) according to different codes' (Lambert and Robyns' definition). It is a form of 'cannibalism.' Yet this term is not to be understood as another form of possessing the original, but as a liberating form, one which eats, digests, and frees oneself from the original. Cannibalism is to be understood not in the Western sense *i.e.* that of capturing, dismembering, mutilating, and devouring, but in a sense which shows respect, *i.e.*, as a symbolic act of taking back out of love, of absorbing the virtues of a body through a transfusion of blood. Translation is seen as an empowering act, a nourishing act, an act of affirmative play that is very close to the Benjamin/Derrida position, which sees translation as a life-force that ensures a literary text's survival (Gentzler 192).

We have come a long way from taking translation, first as 'carry over of meaning,' and then, as a linguistic activity, which is hinged upon a theory of language, to the present position of accepting it as an 'intracultural activity.' It is identical to culture. Translation is now viewed as 'transformation' and transposition of culture rather than as a purely linguistic activity. The theories of Translation run parallel to literary and critical theories in our time and translation is now considered as a tool of studying comparative literature. Translation theories in recent years have succeeded in giving translation the status of a discipline worthy of academic interest.

## WORKS CITED

Arnold, Matthew. "On Translating Homer." *Essays by Matthew Arnold*. London: OUP, 1914.

Bassnett-McGuire, Susan. *Translation Studies*. London: Routledge, 1991.

Catford, J.C. *A Linguistic Theory of Translation*. London: OUP, 1969.

Das, Bijay Kumar. *The Horizon of Translation Studies*. New Delhi: Atlantic Publishers, 1998.

Devy, G.N. *In Another Tongue: Essays on Indian English Literature.* Madras: Macmillan, 1995.

Engle, Paul and H.N. Engle. Foreword. *Writing from the World II.* Iowa City: University of Iowa Press, 1985.

Gentzler, Edward. *Contemporary Translation Theories.* London: Routledge, 1993.

Holmes, James, S. *et al.* ed. *The Nature of Translation.* The Hague: Mouton, 1970.

Jakobson, Roman. "On Linguistic Aspect of Translation," *On Translator* ed. R.A. Brower. Cambridge Mass: Harvard Press, 1999.

Kermode, Frank. *Continuities.* London: Routledge and Kegan Paul, 1968.

Lefevere, Andre. *Translating Poetry: Seven Strategies and a Blue Print.* Assen/Amsterdam: Ven Garcum, 1975.

Longfellow, Henry Wadsworth. *Dante into English.* Ed. William J. De Sua. Chapel Hill: University of North Carolina Press, 1964.

Nida, Eugene, A. *Toward a Science of Translating.* Leiden: E.J. Brill, 1964.

Niranjana, Tejaswini. *Siting Translation.* Hyderabad: Orient Longman Ltd., 1992.

Quine, Willard V.O. *Word and Object.* Cambridge, M.A.: The MIT Press, 1960.

Richards, I.A. "Toward a Theory of Translating." *Studies in Chinese Thought.* Ed. A.F. Wright Chicago: University of Chicago Press, 1953.

Steiner, George. *After Babel.* New York: OUP, 1975.

Talgeri, Pramod and S.B. Verma, Ed. *Literature in Translation.* Bombay: Popular Prakashan, 1988.

Will, Frederick. *The Knife in the Stone.* The Hague: Mouton, 1973.

# 12

# Translation Theory and Practice: The Indian Context

Translation comes after the original and is dependent on it. Hence, it is secondary to the original. To translate is to put an original text to a process of decoding and find out an equivalent of it in the target language through the process of recording. This is what Roman Jakobson tells us about the process of translation. In the West, translation used to be considered as secondary and inferior to the original. This is not the case in India.

In India Sanskrit was the source language and texts written in it were considered as source language texts (SL Texts). The Indian literary tradition is full of rendering of Sanskrit texts into regional languages (*i.e.*, 'Bhas̄a' languages G.N. Devy's term). But we never call them translations and always regarded them as new writings (*i.e.,* original texts). That is why, translation is taken as new writing in India. As Sujit Mukherjee has rightly put it:

> This can be demonstrated most easily in the career of the *Mahabharata* and the *Ramayana* in various Indian languages. The *Pampabharata* and the *Pandavavijaya*, for example, are complete and self-contained literary works, irrespective of their sources. But when literary historians tell us that Pampa 'wrote' the *Mahabharata* in Kannada or that Kashiram Das 'wrote' the same in Bangla, we were suddenly made aware that 'writing' in this context is not divorced from the act of original composition. (Cygnus 5)

Western translation theorists lay emphasis on translation's faithfulness or fidelity to the original, though sometimes they also concede the freedom of the translation from the original. In India translation is known as 'Rupantar' meaning 'Change in form,' or 'Bhasantar' meaning in 'another language' or 'Anuvad' meaning 'coming after' or 'following after.' Translation for Indians is 'after life' or a 'new life' and therefore, it need not be 'faithful' to the original. Sri Aurobindo reinforces this point when he says:

> A translator is not necessarily bound to the original he chooses; he can make his own poem out of it, if he likes, and that is what is generally done. (Nandakumar 65)

R.S. Pathak has outlined the status of translation in India in the following words:

> There was almost no tradition of translation in ancient India in its modern sense except for '*bhashya*' and '*Teeka*' which can be considered translation in its very loose sense. But both of them were practiced in the same language. Barring a brief affair with translation through Burzoe's translation of *Panchtantra* in Pahalvi language in the sixth century and then by Abdullah Ibnal Mofka in Arabic there were not many translations from non-Indian to Indian languages. The poets of the Bhakti period in India were translators in a different and loose sense, as they strove to translate ancient Indian knowledge and wisdom manifested in different treatises through Sanskrit by appropriating it in various Indian *bhashas*. In the second half of the 17th century Dara Shikoh's translations of the *Upanishadas* from Sanskrit into Persian deserve particular mention here. But the real impetus to translation activities was given in the British colonial period, though most of them were not free from colonial/ political considerations. Excepting translation of some ancient Indian classics and treatises into Western languages most of the translations were into Indian languages and the works selected for translations from the Western (English) to Indian languages were such as would serve their (colonizer's) purposes. If translations of Khayyam's *Rubaiyats* and even some of the Indian literary classics were attempted to exoticize

> the Orient to the West, then the translations by William Carey and company were motivated more by religious expansionist intentions than by 'catholicity' of Christianity. Translations from English to Indian languages in the subsequent years crushed and 'complexed' Indian creative sensibility, though there is no denying the fact that they helped in introducing some new literary trends and movements in Indian literatures. (V-VI)

Translation practice in India varies from period to period. Translation was a kind of new writing in the pre-colonial period and during the colonial period, it came heavily under the influence of the British translators and writers. G.N. Devy gives a clear picture of it in the following words:

> In the Indian context literary translations can be divided into three types: (i) those interested in preserving the ancient literary heritage, (ii) those interested in 'Westernising' Indian languages and literature, and (iii) those interested in 'nationalising' literature in modern Indian languages. In correspondence with the different objectives of these three types their mode of operation differs. (149)

If in the pre-colonial days Sanskrit texts used to be rendered into several Bhāsa languages (we have new versions of the *Ramayana* and the *Mahabharata* in different regional languages of India), during the colonial period it is the English texts, which were translated into regional languages of India. Translation theory during the colonial days emphasized that the translator should translate into the mother tongue from the foreign language. The 'self is the target culture' (*i.e.*, home culture) and the source is the 'other' or foreign culture. According to this rule, Shakespeare, Walter Scott and Byron were translated into Indian languages plentily. G.N. Devy brings out the difference between translations from Sanskrit and translations from English into Bhāsa languages in the following passage:

> The difference between the medieval translations/renderings from Sanskrit and those attempted during the colonial period was that the medieval translations aimed at liberating the society, whereas the colonial translations were merely

'reactionary.' They came either as a reaction to the colonial situation that had hurt the national pride of India, or as imitations of Indological translations of Sanskrit works by scholars like Sir William Jones, Max Muller and others. By the end of the First World War the Indian cultural scene started changing rapidly. A large number of Indian soldiers had returned home after getting an exposure to European cultures other than the British. Also, Mahatma Gandhi had entered the political scene in India creating a new national awareness. A result of these changes was that Indian translators turned now to European literature as well as to literature in other Indian languages. That is how, during the three decades of the Gandhian freedom struggle, interlingual exchange within Indian languages multiplied. Tagore's works, for instance, were translated into many Indian languages. So were Prem Chand's, K.M. Munshi's and V.S. Khandekar's. (150-51)

This is corroborated by K. Ayyappa Paniker when he says:

The 19th century favoured the globalization of culture and as part of the process translation came to acquire a good deal of importance. A few decades after the works of Kalidasa were translated into European languages, they came to be translated into modern Indian languages—about the same time as the works of Shakespeare began to be translated into Indian languages. The growing familiarity of Indian readers with the works of European authors is clearly indicated by the history of translations. English texts led the way; French, German and Russian followed; translations from Asian languages are even now very rare. Latin American works get translated because they are written in European languages. African English writings get precedence over writings in African languages. Contemporary Arabic and Persian literature is still to gain access to the Indian readership. The reception of translated literature is an index to the broadening of literary taste. (130-31)

During the postcolonial period (*i.e.*, Post-Independence era) there is a shift in emphasis in the practice of translation in India. If during the colonial period, English texts and authors were frequently and even, randomly translated into Indian languages, in the postcolonial period, Indian Bhasa language authors and Bhasa language texts are being translated into English with a view to reaching a larger audience.

Here is a paradoxical situation. There is an inherent competition and even conflict between Indian Bhasa language writers and Indian English writers as to who represents true India in their works. Bhasa language writers run down Indian English writers on the ground that the latter are inauthentic for they don't represent the true Indian spirit and English is a foreign language and so on. And what is worse, is that according to Bhasa language writers Indian English writers write with the foreign readers in view and they tend to interpret India to the West. But this is not a fact. Indian English writers are as authentic and sensible as the Indian Bhasa language writers are or supposed to be. They also write in a live idiom (*i.e.*, Indian English, the language that educated Indians speak and write in our country) and moreover, one can't be a lesser Indian if he writes in Engish—a language we have adopted as our own—and greater Indian if he writes in Bhasa language. What about the bilingual writers like Manoj Das, Kamala Das, Jayanta Mahapatra and a few others? What about the self-translators like Rabindranath Tagore and Girish Karnad? Do they become less authentic when they write in English and more authentic when they write in or transcreate into English? The paradox is that most of the well-known Bhasa language writers want to get translated into English. As a result of which we have a vast body of literature called Indian literature in English translation in our country. A.K. Ramanujan, an Indian English poet and a translator par excellence has translated a vast body of Kannada literature into English. The works of Prem Chand, Tagore, U.R. Annathamurthy, Gopinath Mohanty, Vijay Tendulkar to name a few, are all available in English Translation. The translation practice in India is now more from Bhasa literatures into English than from English literature into Indian languages. Comparing the Indian tradition of translation with the West, Sujit Mukherjee says,

> Bible translation has provided the western world with an infinitely rich wealth of practice in translating an older

> text—which is an frequently religious in intention as it is literary in effect. We have no comparable experience in India, although parts of the *Vedas,* much of the *Gita*, many poems of the *Therigatha*—any of these could have served the same purpose. If we were to start now, the consciously secular outlook we have adopted as national policy would persuade us to choose not a religious text but a body of literary works to translate over and over again into all our languages, and derive the kind of benefit which translating the Bible has given to its translators and scholars. Something of this nature did happen around 1961 as part of the centenary celebrations of the birth of Rabindranath Tagore, when more of his writings got translated into more Indian languages than ever before. The Rabindranath canon is large enough for several generations to remain engaged in the task if it is ever to be completed. But there is ample material available already for studying the nature of translation in India of the work of one modern Indian poet. (*Translation as Discovery* 81)

In Indian Universities Translation Studies is offered as a course at the Master's level. And what is more, practical translation—that is, translation of a regional classic is now being considered to be a fit subject for the award of a Ph.D degree in some Indian Universities. Since critical theories are now studied in India with interest and enthusiasm, Translation Studies as a discipline has become a favourite with Indian academics. Moreover, the study of Comparative Literature in India has also contributed immensely to the study of Translation theory and practice in recent times. In the Indian multilingual and multicultural context, translation plays a vital role for the cause of nation-building. To conclude, I should say that translation activities in India (both theory and practice) can stand comparison with the West particularly in the field of literary translation (*i.e.,* translation of literature).

## WORKS CITED

Devy, G.N. *In Another Tongue.* Madras: Macmillan, 1993.

Mukherjee, Sujit. "Translation as New Writing." *Cygnus* 2: 2 (1981).

___. *Translation as Discovery and Other Essays.* New Delhi: Allied Publishers, 1981.

Nandakumar, Prema. "Translation: A Creative Process." *Cygnus* 2:2 (1981).

Paniker, K. Ayyappa. "The Anxiety of Authenticity: Reflections on Literary Translation." *Indian Literature* 37:4 (1994).

Pathak, R.S. "Editor's Note." *Critical Practice* 1:2 (1994).

# 13

# Comparative Literature and Translation Studies: A Correlation

Comparative Literature is a subject and to some critics it is a non-subject. Its existence depends a lot on translation. In the twenty-first century the study of Comparative Literature is hinged upon the art of translation and translation studies. Translation Studies as a discipline promotes the cause of Comparative Literature in our time. In this chapter an attempt has been made to trace the origin and growth of Comparative Literature *vis-à-vis* the growth of translation studies across the globe.

Comparative Literature owes its origin and title to a series of French anthologies published in 1816 under the title *Cours de Litterature Comparee*. Ulrich Weissterin opines that either Jean-Jacques Ampere or Abel Francois Villemain, "must be regarded as the true father of a systematically conceived Comparative Literature in France—or anywhere, for that matter" (*Comparative Literature and Literary Theory*, 171). If the term "Comparative Literature" came to be used in France in 1820s and 1830s, the German use of the term "Vergleichende Literaturgeschichtre" first occurred in 1854 in a book by Moriz Carriere. And the credit of first using the term in English goes to Matthew Arnold who popularised it in England through his lectures in 1848 and 1857.

In 1900 Ferdinand Brunetiere has observed:

> ...the history of Comparative Literature will sharpen in each one of us, French or English, or German the understanding of the most national characteristics of our great writers. We establish ourselves only in opposing; we are defined only by

> comparing ourselves to others; and we don't know ourselves when we know only ourselves. (Schultz and Rhein 153-82)

This observation brings to our mind the famous line of Kipling's poem, "The English Flag": "And what should they know of England who only England know?" Matthew Arnold made it amply clear in his Inaugural Lecture at Oxford in 1857 when he said:

> Everywhere there is connection, everywhere there is illustration. No single event, no single literature is adequately comprehended except in relation to other events, to other literatures. (*On the Modern Element in Literature*)

Comparative Literature is a reaction against narrow nineteenth century nationalism. The best example of narrow nationalism and imperialism is evident in Thomas Babington Macauley's statement made in 1935:

> I have never found one among them (Orientalists) who could deny that a single shelf of a good European library was worth the whole native literature of India and Arabia. I have certainly never met with any Orientalist who ventured to maintain that the Arabic and Sanskrit poetry could be compared to that of the great European nations. (Curtin 178-79)

As Susan Bassnett has rightly pointed out that "Comparative Literature seems to have emerged as an antidote to nationalism, even though its roots went deep into national cultures" (21). If Comparative Literature is a reaction against narrow nationalism in the West, in India it is directly linked with the rise of modern Indian nationalism. Comparative Literature is an assertion of national as well as cultural identity in the Indian context. If G.N. Devy links the growth of Comparative Literature to the rise of nationalism in the modern period in India, Swapan Majumdar links it with National Literature. Majumdar said:

> ...it is because of this predilection for National Literature—much deplored by the Anglo-American critics as a methodology—that Comparative Literature has struck roots in the Third World nations and in India in particular. (53)

Comparative Literature Studies gained momentum in the West with the establishment of chairs in the West. Chairs of Comparative Literature were set up at Harvard in 1890 and Lyon in 1897. As Susan Bassnett puts it:

> Indeed, it is in the last two decades of the nineteenth century that Comparative Literature began to be established internationally, for in addition to the subject being taught in institutions of higher education in Europe and the United States, Hutcheson Macauley Posnett, Professor of Classics and English Literature at University College, Auckland, New Zealand, published in a full length study of the subject, entitled *Comparative Literature* in 1886, and two journals were founded in Europe. (22)

Comparative Literature is a study of intertextuality. For instance, if we have to compare a novel of English with that of an Oriya novel we have to use either English or Oriya as the medium. But if we have to compare a French novel (the language we don't know), we have to read first an English version of French novel and then compare it with an Oriya novel and use either English or Oriya, the two languages we know as the medium of our assessment. What I suggest here is that it is through translation we read the literature written in a language which we don't know and therefore, translation becomes a tool for the study of Comparative Literature. Translation brings intertextuality to our knowledge and that intertextuality is the core of Comparative Literature. Having said so, let us examine how Translation Theories and Studies have altered our idea of the differences between the original and the translated text in recent times. It is in the 1960s Translation Studies gained momentum is U.S.A. and U.K. In 1964 Paul Engle, Director Writers' Workshop at the University of Iowa organised the first translation workshop. In 1965 Ted Hughes and Daniel Weissbort published *Modern Poetry in Translation* and in 1968 National Translation Centre published its first issue of *Delos*—a journal devoted to history and aesthetics of translation.

Evan-Zohar, the leader of the translation theorists from Tel Aviv in a paper titled, "Translation Theory Today" has questioned the validity of the superiority of the original over the translation. This is how Evan-Zohar puts it:

> How many times have we been tortured by the cliches of the uninitiated, veteran or novice, that translation is never equal to the original, that languages differ from one another, that culture is 'also' involved with translation procedures, that when a translation is 'exact' it tends to be 'literal' and hence loses the 'spirit' of the original, that the 'meaning' of a text means both 'content' and 'style,' and so on. Not to speak of such approaches where norms are either overtly or covertly stated, *i.e.* where we are told how translations should look or how they should be conceived of in terms of one or another evaluative norm. (*Poetics Today* 2:4:1-7)

In an age, when it is believed that the definitive text belongs only to religion or fatigue, the post-structuralists have done well to underline the fallacy of believing in a single and definitive reading of a text, a work of translation cannot be dismissed as inferior to the original or even, secondary to the primary text. The earlier notion of translation being unfaithful to the original was questioned by Feminist Translation Theorists, led by Lori Chamberlain. Referring to the sexualization of the translation terminology, Chamberlain points out that it appears:

> ...perhaps most familiarly in the tag 'les belles infideles' like women, the adage goes, translations should be either beautiful or faithful. The tag is made possible both by the rhyme in French and by the fact that the word 'traduction' is a feminine one, thus making 'les beaux infideles' impossible. This tag owes its longevity—it was coined in the seventeenth century—to more than phonetic similarity; what gives it the appearance of truth is that it has captured a cultural complicity between the issues of fidelity in translation and in marriage. For 'les belles infideles,' fidelity is defined as an implicit contract between translation (as woman) and original (as husband, father, or author). However, the infamous 'double standard' operates here as it might have in traditional marriage: the 'unfaithful' wife/translation is publicly tried for crimes the husband/original is by law incapable of committing. This contract, in short, makes it impossible for

> the original to be guilty of infidelity. Such an attitude betrays real anxiety about the problem of paternity and translation; it mimics the patrilineal kinship system where paternity—not maternity—legitimizes an offspring. (Venuti, *Rethinking Translation* 57-74)

Lori Chamberlain has drawn our attention to 'Cultural Complicity' between fidelity in translation and in marriage. She was supported by Feminist translation theorists like Susan Bassnett, Barbara Johnson, Barbara Godard, Sherry Simon and Annie Brisset, who used metaphors of 'infidelity' in the 1980s.

In the 1970s the Tel-Aviv Group propounded polysystem theory and in 1980s the Feminist translation theorists have questioned the supremacy of the original over the translation. Susan Bassnett has highlighted the contribution of Evan-Zohar to translation studies in the following words:

> The way in which translation studies began to mount an offensive against the dominance of the original and the consequent relegation of translation to a position of subservience was initially through the work of Evan-Zohar and his colleagues, most notably Gideon Toury, on Polysystems theory. For Evan-Zohar went much further than simply attacking the vagueness of the language surrounding translation. He noted that although translation appeared to have played a major role in the development of national cultures, this fact was almost ignored by historians of culture, and there was practically no research at all on the function of translated literature within a literary system. The Renaissance, for example, has generally been perceived as a time of intensive translation activity, yet any systematic assessment of what was translated, why, by whom and how had not taken place. (*Comparative Literature* 141)

In a culture and society certain conditions determine high translation activity. Evan-Zohar suggests that high translation activity takes place when a literature is in its initial stage of development or when a literature perceives itself to be marginal. Furthermore, when there are crises or turning points in a culture, the translation activity gains momentum. For example, in the twelfth century Europe the translation activity was significant because of a shift from epic to romance. In India the two great epics—the *Ramayana* and the *Mahabharata*—were translated (should we say, transcreated?) into several regional languages to fill the vacuums in respective Bhasa literatures (*i.e.*, regional Indian literatures). It is through translation we transform one literature into another and the more we translate, the more we get the opportunity of comparing different literary texts.

In India there is a craze for translation in recent times for two reasons. First, writers and critics of one literature (say, Oriya literature, or Hindi literature and so on) want their literature to be translated into English or any other regional language of the country for the purpose of bringing it into the notice of all India readers. Secondly when a literature is translated into a target language, it immediately gets the scope of being compared with the literary texts written originally in the target language. Translation is a kind of transformation (or should we say 'regulated transformation' as Derrida would make us believe?).

In the post-1980 period, translation has been given a position equal to that of the original by such critics and translators like Lambert, Van Gorp, Theo Hermans, Walter Benjamin, Jacques Derrida, Haroldo and Augusto de Campos, Helene Cixous and a few others. From Polysystem theory of the 1970s we have come a longway to 'Cannibalistic' theory which radically alters our views of translation. By hindsight we know that translation theories have depended upon some notion of equivalence such as linguistic, structural and dynamic between the source text and the target text (or between original and translation). Evan-Zohar and Guideon Toury have deviated from this position by treating translation in terms of actual product rather than an ideal faithful version of the original. Deconstructionists go a step ahead by saying that the 'original' is also a work of translation of thoughts and ideas and hence there is no vital difference between the original and the translation. Edwin Gentzler has given a clear picture of Deconstructionist view of translation in the following passage:

> The subject of translation theory has traditionally involved some concept of determinable meaning that can be transferred

> to another system of signification. Deconstruction questions such a definition of translation and uses the practice of translation to demonstrate the instability of its own theoretical framework. Deconstruction resists systems of categorization which separate "source" text from "target" text of "language" from "meaning," denies the existence of underlying forms independent of language, and questions theoretical assumptions which presume originary beings, in whatever shape or form. In translation, what is visible is language referring not to things, but to language itself. Thus the chain of signification is one of infinite regress—the translated text becomes a translation of another earlier translation and translated words, although viewed by deconstructionists as "material" signifiers, represent nothing but other words representing nothing but still other words representing. (147)

The importance of Derrida's theory of translation lies in the fact that he does not consider the source text 'original' because it is an elaboration of an idea, of a meaning, in other words, it is in itself a translation. The logical consequences of Derrida's argument about the status of translation is to do away with the dichotomy between original and translation, and thereby put an end to the view that relegates translation to a secondary position.

*The Manipulation of Literature* (1985) edited by Theo Hermans gives a new direction to translation studies. In this book an attempt has been made to show translation as 'a primary manipulative textual strategy.' It is a step ahead of polysystems theory of structuralist origin which challenges the supremacy of the original over the translation, for it is 'concerned with mapping,' 'with tracing patterns of translation activity at a given point of time.' Translation, in the post-structuralist stage is treated as a process of textual manipulation in which 'the concept of plurality replaces dogmas of faithfulness to a source text.' Hence, the idea of 'original' is challenged as Derrida has done from a variety of perspectives.

In the 1990s, translation theorists such as Jose Lambert and Clem Robyns have shifted the emphasis of translation studies from semiotic model to intercultural activity. Translation has become identical to culture. Edwin Gentzler sums up the views of Lambert and Robyns in the following words:

> Translation gets defined by Lambert and Robyns as the "migrations—through—transformation of discursive elements (signs)" and as the "process during which they are interpreted (re-contextualized) according to different codes. Translations thus take place not only between fixed languages and national literatures, but also between any sort of competing or varying discourses." (186)

Recently new theories of translation are propounded by the translators in Brazil and Canada. Haroldo and Augusto de Campos are the principal theoreticians and practitioners of cannibalistic concept of translation. They want to erase the boundary between the source and target texts. "The images of translation as cannibalism, and vampirism whereby the translator sucks out the blood of the source text to strengthen the target text, as transfusion of blood that endows the receiver with new life, can all be seen as radical metaphors that spring from post-modernist translation theory" (Bassnett 155). This supports the Polysystem theory and Deconstructionist theory of the rejection of the power hierarchy which privileged the source text over the translated text and relegates the translator to a secondary place. Else Viera underlines the significance of cannibalistic theory in the following passage:

> The cannibalistic translational philosophy of nourishing from two reservoirs, the source text, and the target literature, and to the same extent, the reverse reading of translation operated by Benjamin and Derrida exposes a number of epistemological questions that traditional traductology is unfit to answer. Or, using Benjamin's terms, traditional traductology demands a translation, a revision...if, in the cannibalist, philosophy, translation becomes a two-way flow, the very terminology 'source' and 'target' becomes depleted. By the same token, the power relation between source and target, superior/inferior ceases to exist. (155)

Cannibalism should be understood in the sense of a liberating form and freeing the translation from the original but not as another form of possessing the original. As Edwin Gentzler has rightly put it:

> Cannibalism is to be understood not in the Western sense, *i.e.*, that of capturing, dismembering, mutilating, and devouring, but in a sense which shows respect, *i.e.*, as a symbolic act of taking back out of love, of absorbing the virtues of a body through a transfusion of blood. Translation is seen as an empowering act, a nourishing act, an act of affirmative play that is very close to the Benjamin/Derrida position, which sees translation as a life-force that ensures a literary text's survival. (192)

In Canada, the translation is seen from feminine perspective in the mid-1980s and the translation theorists have built upon Helene Cixous' notion of 'in-betweenness' for 'feminine' writing takes place 'in between two poles of male and female.' This concept is clearly explained by Nicole Ward-Jouve in the following passage:

> The translator is a being in-between. Like words in translation, s/he endlessly drifts between meanings. S/he tries to be the go-between, to cunningly suggest what readings there could be in the foreign language other than those the chosen translation makes available.... You are led to reflect on how particular translations become constructed. What gets lost, what is gained, what and how altered, in the passage from one language to the next. (47)

If the binary notion of translation in the past took original and translated texts as two poles which are interpreted in terms of masculine and feminine respectively, the feminist translation theory by emphasizing on the notion of in-betweenness, 'reconstructs the space in which the translation takes place as bi-sexual, belonging neither to one or to the other.'

Translation process involves two activities simultaneously —reading and writing. That is why Kathy Mezei describes translation process as 'a compound act of reading and writing' and the translator as both reader and writer. Susan Bassnett aptly sumps up the achievement of the Brazilian and the Canadian groups of translation theorists in the following passage:

> The Brazilian and the Canadian groups of translation theorists have in common the aim of celebrating the role of the translator, of making the translator visible in an act of transgression that seeks to reconstruct the old patriarchal/European hierarchies. Translation seen in their terms is indeed a political activity, and one of the utmost importance. Haroldo and Augusto de Campos use translation as a way of affirming their right as Brazilians to reread and repossess canonical European literature, while the Canadian women see translation as fundamental to their existence as bilinguals and as feminists struggling against phallo/logocentric values. Both groups are concerned to find a translation practice and terminology that will convey the rupture with the dominance of the European heritage even as it is transmitted. In their different ways, one group with the metaphoric language of blood and death, the other with a series of metaphors deriving from the notion of the "mother tongue" are proposing a post colonial notion of translation, which contests the old imperialist view. (157-58)

Translation has come a long way from mere imitation of the original to a 'compound act of reading and writing' simultaneously. And it has emerged as a discipline in recent years. The use of translation is invaluable in the study of Comparative Literature in the multilingual and multicultural context. Susan Bassnett and Lefevere have emphasized this in the following words:

> With the development of Translation Studies as a discipline in its own right, with a methodology that draws on comparatistics and cultural history, the time has come to think again. Translation has been a major shaping force in the development of world culture and no study of comparative literature can take place without regard to translation. (160)

Translation has proven as a major factor for the development of culture all over the world. As a discipline it has attracted the attention of translators and scholars everywhere in the late twentieth and early twenty-first century. It brings a correlation between literature and culture in every multilingual and cultural society. Hence, translation highly promotes the cause of comparative literature. That is the reason why Bassnett has suggested that, "We should look upon translation studies as the principal discipline from now on, with Comparative Literature as a valued but subsidiary subject area" (161).

## WORKS CITED

Arnold, Matthew. *On the Modern Element in Literature.* Inaugural Lecture delivered in the University of Oxford, 14 November 1857.

Bassnett, Susan. *Comparative Literature: A Critical Introduction.* Oxford: Blackwell Publishers Ltd., 1998.

Bassnett, Susan and Andre Lefevere. Eds. *Translation, History and Culture.* London: Pinter, 1990.

Brunetiere, Ferdinand. "European Literature." *Comparative Literature: The Early Years.* Eds. Joachim Schultz and Phillip Rhein. Chapel Hill: University of North Carolina Press, 1973.

Chamberlain, Lori. "Gender and Metaphorics of Translation." *Rethinking Translation.* Ed. Lawrence Venuti. London: Routledge, 1992.

Curtin, Philip D., Ed. *Imperialism: The Documentary History of Western Civilization.* New York: Walker Co., 1971.

Evan-Zohar, Itamar. "Translation Theory Today." *Poetics Today.* 2: 4 Summer/Autumn, 1981.

Gentzler, Edwin. *Contemporary Translation Theories.* London: Routledge, 1993.

Hermans, Theo., Ed. *The Manipulation of Literature.* London: Croom Helm, 1985.

Majumdar, Swapan. *Comparative Literature: Indian Dimensions.* Calcutta: Papyrus, 1987.

Remak, Henry. "Comparative Literature, Its Definition and Function." *Comparative Literature: Method and Perspective.* Eds. Newston Stalknecht and Horse Frenz: Carbondale. Southern Illinois Press, 1961.

Ward-Jouve, Nicole. "To Fly/to Steal, no More? Translating French Feminisms into English." *While Woman Speaks with Forked Tongue: Criticism as Autobiography.* London: Routledge, 1991.

Weisstein, Ulrich. *Comparative Literature and Literary Theory.* Bloomington: Indian University Press, 1973.

# 14

# Translation in the Twenty-First Century: The Global Context

Modern Translation theory in the West owes its origin to the first Translation Workshop in U.S.A. in 1964. It was Paul Engle, Director of the Writers' Workshop at the University of Iowa, who hired a full-time director for the Translation Workshop and gave academic credit to literary translations. Prior to it, I.A. Richards in his essay, "Toward a Theory of Translating" published in 1953 had suggested how one should compare translated texts to original texts. As Edwin Gentzler has rightly suggested that, "'Modern' translation theory, like current literary theory begins with structuralism and reflects the proliferation of the age" (2). In recent years translation theory has exploded with developments from purely linguistic approach of the 1960s through the Polysystem theory and deconstruction in the 1970s to the culture based theory in the closing two decades of the twentieth century. Translation like literary criticism has become culture based in recent years.

In the twenty-first century as in the 1980s and 1990s culture has become mixed—*i.e.*, hybrid, all over the world. Access to the internet has made it possible to see events taking place immediately. Satellite dishes, cable connections have bridged both time and space. One can see the events happening in the world sitting in his drawing room 'live.' Not only that all cultures have become mixed and hybrid—nothing is pure. In the past, we in India according to our tradition never uttered the names of the elders before them—*i.e.*, we never addressed them by their first names. And now, because of the influence of the

West and popularity of television programmes and interviews, we address the elders by their first names. I am not saying that it is either good or bad. What I emphasize here is that culturally the countries of the world are getting closer and united. Moreover, what happens in the West, is imitated (at least, followed) in India and what happens in New Delhi is followed in other state capitals even in remote villages. This is due to the influence of the media. Globalization is taking place rapidly. Paul St. Pierre draws our attention to this aspect in the following passage:

> There is no question that the development, and consolidation, of the media worldwide is of major importance today. When staying in a hotel in India in 2001, I could watch the gameshow 'Crorepati,' with an Indian superstar as host. Contestants were selected on the basis of how quickly they could answer a 'skill'—testing question; they then proceeded to a question and answer session with the host, with the amount they could win increasing exponentially. They had the possibility of calling on their friends, on the audience, or even on the computer for help. 'Crorepati' was the Indian version of the American gameshow 'Who wants to be a millionaire?,' with the same format, the same music and the same set. Beyond the similarities between the American and Indian versions, the differences too are significant: the folksy demeanor of the American host was replaced by a more reserved, somewhat paternalistic, approach in India, and the amount to be won was no longer the mythical American sum of one million dollars, but the Indian amount of a crore of rupees. Globalization, yes, but also adaptation to local realities. (99)

As the world is sinking, 'nativism' and 'nationality' are slowly but constantly yielding place to globalisation. The cultural barrier is breaking down. Edward Said has drawn our attention to this aspect of human civilization in the concluding paragraph of *Culture and Imperialism* in the following words:

> No one today is purely one thing. Labels like Indian, or woman, or Muslim, or American are no more than starting-points which, if followed into actual experience for only a moment, are quickly left behind. Imperialism consolidated

> the mixture of cultures and identities on a global scale. But its worst and most paradoxical gift was to allow people to believe that they were only, mainly, exclusively white, or black, or Western, or Oriental. No one can deny the persisting continuities of long traditions, sustained habitations, natural languages, and cultural geographies, but there seems no reason except fear and prejudice to keep insisting on their separation and distinctiveness as if that was all human life was about. Survival in fact is about connections between things: in Eliot's phrase, reality cannot be deprived of the other echoes [that] inhabit the graden. "It is more rewarding—and more difficult—to think correctly and sympathetically, contrapunctuality, about others than only about us." But this also means no trying to rule others, not trying to classify them or put them in hierarchies, above all not constantly reiterating how our "culture" or "country" is number one (or not number one, for that matter). For the intellectual there is quite enough of value to do without that. (408)

In the changing circumstances, what should be the role of the Translator? What is the future of translation in the 21st century? Translation like Literary and Critical theories has become a discipline in its own right. Translation is re-writing of the original without doing violence to the latter. It is both necessary and useful in bringing different literatures of the world together despite linguistic and cultural differences. Two approaches—one by Feminist Canadian translation theorists and another by Brazilian translation theorists—are likely to gain currency in the 21st century.

Feminist approach to translation studies led by such translation theorists as Susan Bassnett, Barbara Godard, Barbara Johnson in Canada criticise the fidelity theory (*i.e.*, fidel or close to the original) because that makes the original husband or master and translation an unfaithful wife or slave. They pleaded for the re-creation of the original in the work of the translation. Hence, translation is viewed as re-creation. Brazilian translation theorists such as de Campos brothers (Haroldo and Augusto de Campos) view translation as a form of 'transgression'—a kind of postmodern and non-Eurocentric approach to translation. For them, translation is a form of "cannibalism." In the words of Edwin Gentzler, "yet this term is not to be understood as another form of possessing the original, but as a liberating form, one which eats, digests, and frees oneself from the original. Cannibalism is to be understood not in the Western sense, *i.e.*, that of capturing, dismembering, mutilating, and devouring, but in a sense which shows respect, *i.e.*, as a symbolic act of taking back out of love, of absorbing the virtues of a body through a transfusion of blood. Translation is seen as an empowering act, a nourishing act, an act of affirmative play that is very close to the Benjamin/Derrida position, which sees translation as a life-force that ensures a literary text's survival" (192).

Translation is subjected not only to two semiotic systems (source and target languages) but to two different cultures. Translators not only say what the author says, in another language (*i.e.*, target language) but they also say what the original means. In other words, translators re-create the original in the target language. It is in this sense that the translation of literary texts assumes importance. Sherry Simon has drawn our attention to the way translation has been understood in different cultures:

> In the Indian tradition, for example, translation is understood as a form of rewriting, and there are a number of terms used. The Romans, whose culture was essentially translated from Greek, also had a rich vocabulary. They distinguished between stricter and less literal translation, with terms like 'verto,' 'converto,' 'transverto,' 'imitari' (looser forms of translation) and 'interpreter' and 'exprimere' (closer translation), with later additions of 'mutate,' 'transfero' and 'translatare.' (Folena 1994: 8-9)
>
> The medieval vocabulary was even more complex. It distinguished between the kinds of languages involved translating from a noble to a vulgar language, or between vulgar languages—Don Quixote called this "translating among easy languages" (Folena 1994: 13) and the kinds of texts involved (sacred, didactic, legal, historical or poetic). It was presumed that these different kinds of translation would not employ the same methods or seek the same ends. (48-49)

During the process of translation, the language and form of the original change as the work passes from one set of reading based on 'culturally-influenced potential interpretations' to another. Salah Basalamah makes a case for translation in the following words:

> An original text is intimately bound to its context of origin, whereas a translation is but one possible reiteration in another context, emphasizing its *differance* with the original and offering it survival, a new life, a new identity. Thus, with the survival of the original a new text is born—the translation, with its own context and its own meanings. (62)

Having discussed some of the current notions of translation studies, let us turn our attention to the sea change that translation has undergone over the years. Originally translation was undertaken from the 'other' tongue to the mother tongue. For example, we in India used to translate Sanskrit texts into regional languages and during the British period from English into Indian Languages. Now in the postcolonial era, we translate from Indian languages into the languages of the world, particularly into English. We have a vast body of literature called "Indian Literature in English Translation." Similarly the recent theories of translation have altered our idea of translation or translation process. As Alexis Nouss rightly puts it:

> Traditional theories understand translation as a relationship of the 'same' to the 'other.' To translate is to convert difference into similarity, to make the author write as if s/he had written directly in the target language. But alterity is never simply unidirectional. The other does not refer back to the same, or to the other of the same—which is simply an extension or projection of the same—but to a radically different other, a subject constantly changing in its discursivity and historicity. From French Theory to Anglo-Saxon pragmatics, to reflection on the subaltern, the false dichotomy between identity and alterity, self and other, has been definitively broken down. (142)

About translation there are two divergent views: One, those who believe that it is not very faithful to the original (falsifier of the original) say like Brendan Kenney that it is 'the art of fascinating failure' (107) and two, those who believe that it is both true and false say with George Steiner that "Translation is both possible and impossible—a dialectical antinomy characteristic of esoteric argument" (89).

Translation is necessary for the survival of the original beyond its lifetime (that is why, translation is called 'after life') and also outside the source language (*i.e.*, the original language in which it is written). Otherwise, the original will die a natural death. For example, now we read Chaucer's works in translation into Modern English because his language is not intelligible to us. That is how, Chaucer survives in English literature. It is said and rightly so that, 'translate or die.' I would like to cite one anecdote here. There was a man who wanted to see his wife chaste. So he kept her a virgin throughout her life. Then she died and he followed him. That explains the importance of translation. If on the plea of 'fidelity' a text remains untranslated, it will die like the woman in the anecdote.

Just because the original comes before the translation does not mean that the former is superior to the latter. They are complementary to each other. As Alexis Nouss has rightly said:

> The translated text exists through its difference from the original, and the original makes known and legitimizes its own existence only in and through translation. Each refers irremediably to the other. Neither exists completely separately; the existence of each is interwoven—metissage—with that of the other. (146)

The French term 'metissage' means inter-weaving of different linguistic and cultural strands within the same text. Translation becomes a kind of transformation of the original. It moves between two languages and two cultures, playing on the uncertainty of meaning both in source language and target language. Translation brings the gap between two languages and two cultures. I concur with Alexis Nouss' view:

> 'Translated form,' 'translated into'—these expressions confirm the highly ideological expressions of 'source' and 'target' criticized earlier and reproduce the dualistic

> dichotomy. Rather than 'translated from' or 'translated into,' it would be better to speak of 'translated between.' When I translate, I translate as much the other into myself as myself into the other, and through this contact, this exposure, this 'experience of the foreigns,' I find resources in language, and modes of thought and expression which were latent and which I am able to reactivate. I receive the foreigner, who takes refuge in my language but I too take refuge in his. (147)

Thus, the gap between the original and translation has been bridged in recent years. Not only that, translation has been given an equal status with that of the original in the form of Copyright Act being bestowed upon the translation. Salah Basalamah quotes U.S. Copyright Law and Berne Convention to show how translation have been given protection under them.

"U.S. Copyright Law: The copyright in a compilation or derivative work extends only to the material contributed by the author of such work, as distinguished from the pre-existing material employed in the work, and does not imply any exclusive right in the pre-existing material."

Berne Convention: Translations, adaptations, arrangements of music and other alternations of a literary or artistic work shall be protected as original works without prejudice to the copyright in the original work (61).

Translation has been given an independent status by law and translation theories have given new meanings to it. In the twenty-first century, translation will play a major role in bringing the literatures of the world together for the benefit of the mankind. Both for international communication and globalisation, translation will play a crucial role now more than ever before. Translation has become a discipline in its own right and now, as Susan Bassnett and Andre Lefevere have suggested that "perhaps Comparative Literature should be redefined as a 'subcategory of Translation Studies'" (12). The future of Translation Studies in the 21st century is immense.

## WORKS CITED

Basalamah, Salah. "Translation Rights and the Philosophy of Translation: Remembering the Debts of the Original." *Journal of Contemporary Thought* 15 (Summer 2002).

Bassnett, Susan and Andre Lefevere, Eds. *Translation, History and Culture.* London: Pinter, 1990.

Gentzler, Edwin. *Contemporary Translation Theories.* London: Routledge, 1993.

Kennelly, Brendan. "On Translating from Gaelic." *The World of Translation.* New York: P.E.N. American Centre, 1987.

Nouss, Alexis. "Translation and Metissage." *Journal of Contemporary Thought* 15 (Summer 2002).

Said, Edward. *Culture and Imperialism.* London: Chatto and Windus, 1993.

Simon, Sherry. "A Single Brushstroke Writing through Translation: Anne Carson," *Journal of Contemporary Thought* 15 (Summer 2002).

St. Pierre, Paul. "Translation in an Era of Globalization." *Journal of Contemporary Thought* 15 (Summer 2002).

Steiner, George. *After Babel: Aspect of Language and Translation*, London: Oxford University Press, 1975.

# 15

# From Translation of Bhasa Literature to Comparative Literature and Nation Building

At the outset, I propose to explain the key terms in the paper in order to place the subject in its proper context. The concept of translation has undergone a sea change in the postmodern, postcolonial era—particularly in the mid-nineteen eighties, thanks to the proliferation of translation theories. G.N. Devy's term 'bhasa literature' needs an explication, before I say how the translation of it leads to the study of comparative literature and ultimately to nation building.

Translation as an activity was traditionally considered to be inferior—that is, because original writing was considered to be 'superior.' It was never studied seriously and taken as a discipline until mid-sixties. Edward Gentzler underlines five different approaches to translation beginning with mid-sixties till date: (1) American translation workshop, (2) 'Science' of translation, (3) Early translation studies, (4) Polysystem theory and Translation studies, and (5) Deconstruction (2).

Till 1963 there was no translation center, no association of literary translation, no journal exclusive studies in U.S.A. Paul Engle, Director of Writers' Workshop at the University of Iowa, hired a full time director for the first translation workshop in 1964 and gave, as it were, 'a local habitation and a name' to translation studies by recognizing the academic merit of literary translations. In 1965 "the Ford Foundation conferred a $ 150,000 grant on the University Texas at Austin toward the establishment of the National Translation Center." Also in 1965, the first issue of *Modern Poetry in Translation,* edited by Ted Hughes and Daniel Weissbort, was published, providing literary translators a place for their creative work. In 1968, the National Translation Center published the first issue of *Delos,* a journal devoted to the history as well as the aesthetics translation. Literary translation had established a place, albeit a small one, in the production of American culture says Gentzler (8).

In the 1970s, a group of scholars led by Itamar Evan-Zohar from Tel Aviv offered a new perspective on the study of translation. Evan-Zohar and his colleague, Gideon Toury gave us Polysystem theory of translation which challenged the traditional view of 'superiority' of the 'original' and 'infidelity' and 'inferiority' of translation. For Evan-Zohar, translation, far from being a secondary, marginal activity, could be considered as a primary activity. It identifies three cases which accelerates translation activity. One, the early stages of development of a literature, two, when a literature becomes weak or peripheral, and three, when there are crises or literary 'void' in a literature.

Apart from Tel Aviv group, the feminist translation scholars also challenge the view of translation as betrayal of the original. Lori Chamberlain draws the attention of scholars to the sexualization of this terminology: "For 'les belles infideles,' fidelity is defined as an implicit contract between translation (as woman) and original (as husband, father, or author). However, the infamous 'double standard' operates here as it might have in traditional marriage; the 'unfaithful' wife/translation is publicly tried for crimes the husband/original is by law incapable of committing." This contract, in short, makes it impossible for the original to be guilty of infidelity. Such an attitude betrays real anxiety about the problem of paternity and translation; it mimics the matrilineal kinship system where paternity—not maternity—legitimizes an offspring (59).

Chamberlain's emphasis on cultural complicity between fidelity in translation and in marriage finds support from feminist translation scholars such as Susan Bassnett, Barbara Johnson, Barbara Godard, Sherry Simon and others.

*The Manipulation of Literature* (1985) edited by Theo Hermans marks a new stage in the development of translation studies. This shows that there are three distinct phases in the development of translation studies. The first phase, governed by Polysystem theory, challenged the notion of 'superiority' and 'inferiority' between 'original' and 'translation.' In the second phase there is a shift in emphasis from 'original'/'translation' dichotomy to a definite make away from the structuralist origins of Polysystem theory to post-structuralist translation studies. The third phase, "which could be termed the post-structuralist stage, conceives of translation as one of a range of processes of textual manipulation, where the concept of plurality replaces dogmas of faithfulness to a source text, and where the idea of the original is being challenged from a variety of perspective" (Bassnett, 147).

In the 1980s Translation Studies have acquired a new dimension. Translation is no longer viewed as a process of 'change into another language, retaining the sense' or 'substitution of SL textual material in TL,' 'a transference of meaning from SL to TL' but a 'regulated transformation' (Derrida's term). It is again defined as the 'migration through transformation of discursive elements (signs)' and as the 'process during which they are interpreted (re-contextualized) according to different codes' (Lambert and Robyns' definition). It is a form of 'cannibalism.' Yet this term is not to be understood as another form of possessing the original, but as a liberating form, one which eats, digests, and frees oneself from the original. Cannibalism is to be understood not in the Western *i.e.*, that of capturing, dismembering, mutilating, and devouring, but in a sense which shows respect, *i.e.*, as a symbolic act of taking backout of love, of absorbing the virtues of a body through a transfusion of blood. Translation is seen as an empowering act, a nourishing act, an act of affirmative play that is very close to the Benjamin/Derrida position, which sees translation as a life-force that ensures a literary text's survival (Gentzler 192).

Bassnett makes things clear when she says: "The images of translation as cannibalism, as vampirism, whereby the translator sucks out the blood of the source text to strengthen the target text, as transfusion of blood that endows the receiver with new life, can all be seen as radical metaphors that spring from postmodernist postcolonial translation theory. Significantly, they link up with other developments in translation theory discussed above, for what all have in common is a rejection of power hierarchy which privileged the source text relegated the translator to a secondary role" (155).

Translation can never be marginalized. Without it, comparative literature is unthinkable. It deals with two languages which are the basic ingredients of comparative literature. Translation has been a 'major shaping force in the development of world culture.' Translation studies developed as a discipline in its own right in the nineteen eighties.

Having discussed the development of Translation Studies as a discipline, let me explain the term 'Bhasa' in Indian context. It refers to modern Indian languages other than English. For example, Oriya, Bengali, Hindi, etc. are bhasas and literatures in these languages are called bhasa literatures. The translation of one bhasa literature into another bhasa literature provides us an opportunity to make a comparative study between them. In a multi-language country like India, this is inevitable. G.N. Devy makes a valid point in this context: "Literary criticism and literary history in India have been insensitive to the conclusions that can be drawn from a comparative perspective in itself can offer several useful starting points for postulating isolated strands of a theoretical nature about literature in the bhasas, which eventually be gathered into an Indian theory of literature." A blind acceptance of the cliche that Indian culture is eclectic, and the belief that the British came, were seen and immediately accepted, are detrimental to the theory as well as history of literature in India.

It is necessary to remind us that much of literature of the pre-British bhasha period is still a living heritage in India. The poetry of Namadeva (1270-1350) and Tukaram (1598-1650) in Marathi, that of Narasimh Mehta (1408-80) and Akha (1615-75) in Gujarati, of Kabir (1440-1518) and Surdas (1483-1567) in Hindi, of Guru Nanak (1469-1539) in Punjabi, and so on, have formed an inalienable part of the Indian consciousness. Tukaram, Mira,

Kabir and Basaveswar, among others, have been some of the dream-images of India's cultural unconscious. They still guide the hands of modern poets like Arun Kolatkar, A.K. Ramanujan and Gajanan Mahadev Muktibodh. Yet, the cultural amnesia, from which the modern Indian intellectual suffers, creates highly confused attitudes to the period—or periods—of these poets. The common term used to describe the poetry of the above named pre-British poets is bhakti, devotional, or saint poetry. The term covers a vast period extending from the last part of the thirteenth century (Jnanadeva) to the early part of the nineteenth century (Tyaga-raja: 1767-1847). It is like combining European poetry from Dante to Blake under one inexpressive label. It is certainly not very perceptive of literary historians to pack great works from five centuries into a straitjacket of a single insensitive critical category (1992: 42-43).

On the basis of the theoretical framework suggested by Devy, we can study comparative literature in India—that is, Bhakti Movement in Indian Literature and likewise, Dalit literature, after translating bhasa literatures.

Comparative literature is a stage of reading made possible and easier by the availability of translation. René Wellek and Austin Warren have used the term comparative literature in three different senses: first, the study of oral literature, especially of folk-tale themes and their migration, of how and when they have entered 'higher,' 'artistic,' 'literature,' second, comparative literature as "the study of relationships between two or more literatures and the third conception of comparative literature identifies it with the study of literature in its totality, with 'world' literature, with 'general' or 'universal' literature" (47-48).

The study of comparative literature in India can be facilitated on the lines suggested by René Wellek and Warren Austin through translation. In India we have a unique situation—that is, if bhasa literatures are translated into English, a comparative study of such literatures will be easier and fruitful. Instead of translating a bhasa literature into another (say, Oriya into Bangla), we can translate it into English and make a profitable study of it. If 'translation' is literature three, we can have Indian comparative literature in English. That will be the great contribution of translation to literature.

"Translation helps in the process of nation building in our country. The language of our administrative communication at the national level (*i.e.*, by the Central Government) is done either through the official language, or in English. It needs to be translated into more than 20 regional languages for the benefit of the people of several states. Similarly the language of the Court is either English or Hindi and the judgement is delivered in these two languages. Thereafter the judgement is translated into regional languages for the benefit of the common people. For administrative and judiciary purposes, translation is obligatory in India. For the promotion of commerce, trade and industry in our country, we make use of translation. In the modern world, the need for translation is greater than ever before" (Das 83-84). In the international field we need to translate for bilateral talks, and for discussion at the UN and all other international meetings and deliberations. Without translation, it is impossible for world leaders to communicate among themselves.

In this context Paul St Pierre makes a valid observation. "The importance of translation can be located in the fact that translation brings the readers, writers, and critics of one nation into contact with those of others, only in the field of literature, but in all areas of development: science and philosophy, medicine, political science, law and religion, to name but a few. Translation, in this way, plays an essential role in determining how a nation establishes its identity in terms of others, be this through opposition to foreign influences, through assimilation or naturalization of the foreign whereby differences are erased to as great a degree as possible, or through imitation of another, usually dominant culture. These are all different strategies of translation, becoming possibilities at different moments in history and underlying the various types of relation between nations which can exist. There is, thus, a particularly strong interconnection between translation and the constitution of national identity, and the study of translation can be useful—as I will attempt to show later in this paper—in determining the nature of this national identity, and the nature of the relations one nation institutes with others. Seen in this light, translation is a social practice with a definite role to play within a given society, serving in a sense as a form of selection process restricting, conditioning, and in any case modulating cultural immigration. Through translation nations define themselves and in doing so they define others" (qtd. in Das 68-69).

"The translation of literatures in India has assumed a special status in our century. The ancient Indian literary heritage which is to be found in languages like Sanskrit, Prakrit and Apbhransha, etc. can be preserved and even rescued only through translation into English and several regional languages. Indian literature, which is a cover term for all regional literatures of India including Hindi literature, Sanskrit literature and Indian English literature, can reach all the people of India only through translation. In other words, it is through translation that one regional literature can reach the people of region of the country speaking a different language" says, Das (69).

"Translation of world classics into several other languages of the world helps in enriching the target languages. Apart from well-known epics of the world, great authors like Tolstoy and Shakespeare, continue to be translated into several languages. New trends in literature come through translation. The two great epics of India, the *Ramayana* and the *Mahabharata* have been translated into almost all the regional languages of India. That helped the creation of pan-Indian ethos. National myths like 'Laxman Rekha' (*i.e.*, the lines drawn by Laxman, in the *Ramayana* to warn Sita), and 'Bhishma Pratigya' (the oath of Bhishma in the *Mahabharata,* an oath never to be broken) have stirred the minds of the Indians and these myths are available to our people through translations," says Das (71).

"Not only in India but in other parts of the world where multi-lingualism is a reality like France, Canada and Switzerland, translation plays a vital role in nation building. Movements in literature, art and trends in political opinion sail from country to country through translation. The practitioners of translation face great difficulties in translating different culture contexts and linguistic codes and therefore, to translate a text of one county into another is to transform it. In the colonial era, translation was considered to be power. The colonizer used translation as a means to oppress the colonized and the colonized used translation to maintain the indigenous culture and tradition," says Das (73).

To conclude, I would say that translation is an essential factor in the study of comparative literature, which is concerned with patterns of connection of literatures across both time and space. In a multi-lingual and multi-cultural country like India, comparative literature helps in creating an all-India ethos and brings bhasa literatures closer for a meaningful study. And thereby, it furthers the cause of national integration. Thus, the study of translation of bhasa literatures leads to the study of Comparative Literature, reinforces the task of nation building in the Indian context.

## WORKS CITED

Bassnett, Susan. *Comparative Literature: A Critical Introduction.* Oxford: Blackwell, 1988.

Chamberlain, Lori. "Gender and Metaphoric of Translation." *Rethinking Translation.* Ed. Lawrence Venuti. London: Routledge, 1992.

Das, Bijay Kumar. *The Horizon of Translation Studies.* New Delhi: Atlantic Publishers and Distributors, 1998.

Devy, G.N. *After Amnesia.* Hyderabad: Orient Longman, 1992.

Gentzler, Edward. *Contemporary Translation Theories.* London: Routledge, 1993.

Wellek, René and Warren, Austin. *Theory of Literature.* Harmondsworth: Penguin University Books, 1973.

# 16

# Conclusion

In the concluding chapter of the book, I would like to examine some of the leading theories of translation of our time in order to place translation in its proper perspective. That will enable me to define the status of translation. In the second half of the twentieth century the importance of translation has grown by leaps and bounds. This is evident from the number of books published on translation by several scholars. Important and well-known books on translation include Theodore Savory's *The Art of Translation* 1957, R. Brower's *On Translation* 1959, W. Arrowsmith and R. Shatruck's *Craft and Content of Translation* 1961, J.C. Catford's *A Linguistic Theory of Translation* 1965, J. Selver's *The Art of Translating Poetry* 1968, E. Nida & Charles Taber's *The Theory and Practice of Translation* 1969, J. Holmes' ed. *The Nature of Translation* 1970, F.R. Amos' *Early Theories of Translation* 1973, George Steiner's *After Babel* 1975, A. Lefevere's *Translating Poetry* 1975, J. Holmes' *et al.*, ed. *Literature and Translation* 1978, Susan Bassnett-McGuire's *Translation Studies* 1980, Peter Newmark's *Approaches to Translation* 1981, Alan Duff's *The Third Language* 1981 and Gideon Toury's ed. *Translation Across Cultures* 1987. Added to is a number of special numbers on translation studies brought out by leading Indian journals in 1990s. Of these Catford's theory of translation and Nida's theory of translation deserve special mention.

Catford's book, *A Linguistic Theory of Translation* is based on the theory of language. He opines that any theory of translation must draw upon a theory of language—a general linguistic theory. He goes on to elaborate his theory by saying that translation is the replacement of textual material in the source language by an equivalent textual material in the target language. What happens in translation is not the transference of SL meanings into TL but a substitution of TL meanings for SL meanings. Catford means to say that in the realms of translation substitution of meanings takes place but not transference of meanings. Translation equivalence occurs when the SL and TL texts are relatable to the same features of substance. An SL text is translatable to a great degree though not absolutely. Untranslatability occurs when it becomes impossible to build functionally relevant features of the situation into the contextual meaning of the TL text. Catford underlines two types of untranslatability which he terms linguistics and cultural. Susan Bassnett-McGuire explains it in the following words:

> On the linguistic level, untranslatability occurs when there is no lexical or syntactical substitute in the TL for an SL item. So, for example, the German Um wieviel Uhr darf man Sie morgen wecken? or the Danish Jeg fandt brever are linguistically untranslatable, because both sentences involve structures that do not exist in English. Yet both can be adequately translated into English once the rules of English structure are applied. A translator would unhesitatingly render the two sentences as 'What time would you like to be woken tomorrow?' and 'I found the letter,' restructuring the German word order and adjusting the position of the post-positive definite article in Danish to conform to English norms.
>
> Catford's category of linguistic untranslatability, which is also proposed by Popovic, is straightforward, but his second category is more problematic. Linguistic untranslatability, he argues, is due to differences in the SL and the TL, whereas cultural untranslatability is due to the absence in the TL culture of a relevant situational feature for the SL text. He quotes the example of the different concepts of the term bathroom in an English, Finnish or Japanese context, where both the object and the use made of that object are not at all alike. But Catford also claims that more abstract lexical items such as the English term home or democracy cannot be

> described as untranslatable and argues that the English phrases I'm going home or He's at home can 'readily be provided with translation equivalents in most languages' whilst the term democracy is international. (32)

Internationally used terms like 'democracy' and 'home' are hard to define. Culture creates more problems for the translator. Bassnett-McGuire contests the concept of cultural untranslatability in the following way:

> The English phrases can be translated into most European languages and democracy is an internationally used term. But he fails to take into account two significant factors and this seems to typify the problem of an overly narrow approach to the question of untranslatability. If 'I'm going home' is translated as Je vais chez moi, the content meaning of the SL sentence (*i.e.,* self-assertive statement of intention to proceed to place of residence and/or origin) is only loosely reproduced. And if, for example, the phrase is spoken by an American resident temporarily in London, it could either imply a return to the immediate 'home' or a return across the Atlantic, depending on the context in which it is used, a distinction that would have to be spelled out in French. Moreover, the English term home, like the French foyer, has a range of associative meanings that are not translated by the more restricted phrase chez moi. Home, therefore, would appear to present exactly the same range of problems as the Finnish or Japanese bathroom.
>
> With the translation of democracy, further complexities arise. Catford feels that the term is largely present in the lexis of many languages and, although it may be relatable to different political situations, the context will guide the reader to select the appropriate situational features. The problem here is that the reader will have a concept of the term based on his or her own cultural context, and will apply that particularized view accordingly. Hence the difference between the adjective democratic as it appears in the following three phrases is fundamental to three totally different political concepts:

> the American Democratic Party
> the German Democratic Republic
> the democratic wing of the British Conservative Party.
>
> So although the term is international, its usage in different contexts shows that there is no longer (if indeed there ever was) any common ground from which to select relevant situational features. If culture is perceived as dynamic, then the terminology of social structuring must be dynamic also. Lotman points out that the semiotic study of culture not only considers culture functioning as a system of signs, but emphasizes that 'the very relation of culture to the sign and to signification comprises one of its basic typological features.' Catford starts from different premises, and because he does not go far enough in considering the dynamic nature of language and culture, he invalidates his own category of cultural untranslatability. Insofar as language is the primary modelling system within a culture, cultural untranslatability must be *de facto* implied in any process of translation. (32-34)

Catford argues that translation is neither a transference nor a transcoding of meaning but a substitution of meaning. His theory gives a scientific basis to translation studies of our time. Nida has propounded his theory of translation in his essay, "Science of Translation" (483-98) and like Catford has expressed concern about the problem of analysis and transfer of the SL message to the TL. He is of the opinion that translating is basically not a process of matching surface forms by rules of transference but a more complex procedure involving analysis, transfer and restructuring. Translating is reproducing in the receptor language the closest natural equivalent of the message

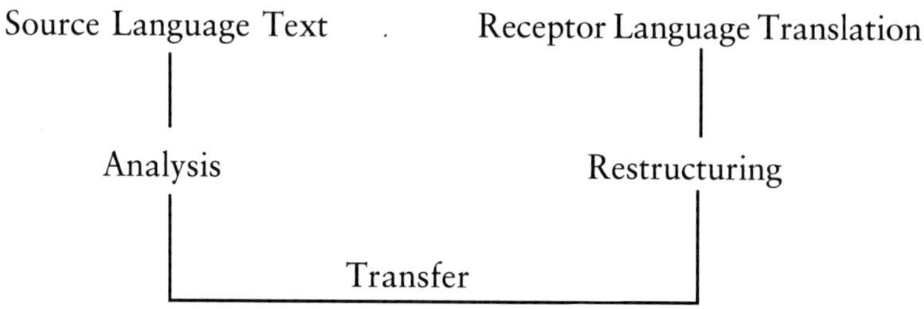

of the source language, first in terms of meaning and second in terms of style. Eugene Nida's model of the translation process can be outlined as shown on p. 164:

> As example of some of the complexities involved in the interlingual translation of what might seem to be uncontroversial items, consider the question of translating yes and hellow into French, German and Italian. This task would seem, at first glance, to be straightforward, since all are Indo-European languages, closely related lexically and syntactically, and terms of greeting and assent are common to all three. For yes standard dictionaries give:
>
> French: oui, si
>
> German: ja
>
> Italian: si
>
> It is immediately obvious that the existence of two terms in French involves a usage that does not exist in the other languages. Further investigation shows that whilst oui is the generally used term, si is used specifically in cases of contradiction, contention and dissent. The English translator, therefore, must be mindful of this rule when translating the English word that remains the same in all contexts.
>
> When the use of the affirmative in conversational speech is considered, another question arises. Yes cannot always be translated into the single words oui, ja or si, for French, German and Italian all frequently double or 'string' affirmatives in a way that is outside standard English procedures (*e.g.*, si, si, si; ja, ja, etc.). Hence the Italian or German translation of yes by a single word can, at times, appear excessively brusque, whilst the stringing together or affirmatives in English is so hyperbolic that it often creates a comic effect.
>
> With the translation of the word hellow, the standard English form of friendly greeting when meeting, the problems are multiplied. The dictionaries give:
>
> French: ca va?; hallo
>
> German: wie geht's; hallo
>
> Italian: ola; pronto; ciao

Whilst English does not distinguish between the words used when greeting someone face to face and that used when answering the telephone, French, German and Italian all do make that distinction. The Italian pronto can only be used as a telephonic greeting, like the German hallo. Moreover, French and German use as forms of greeting brief rhetorical questions, whereas the same question in English *How are you?* or *How do yoú do?* is only used in more formal situations. The Italian ciao, by far the most common form of greeting in all sections of Italian society, is used equally on arrival and departure, being a word of greeting linked to a moment of contact between individuals either coming or going and not to the specific context of arrival or initial encounter. So, for example, the translator faced with the task of translating hello into French must first extract from the term a core of meaning and the stages of the process, following Nida's diagram, might look like this:

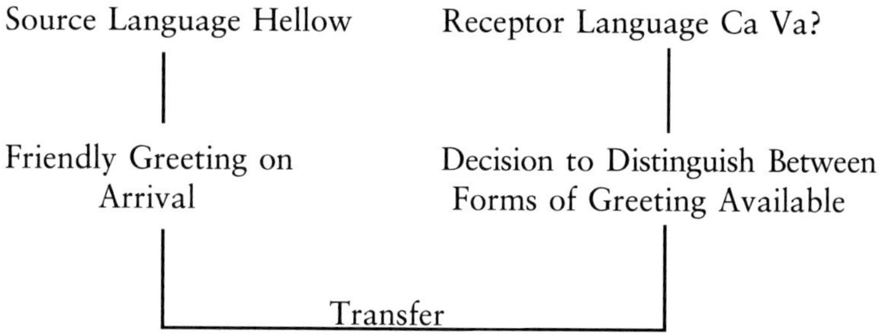


What has happened during the translation process is that the notion of greeting has been isolated and the word hello has been replaced by a phrase carrying the same notion. (qtd. in Bassnett-McGuire 16-18)

Roman Jakobson would describe Nida's conception of translation process as interlingual transposition and Ludskanov would call it semiotic transformation. According to Ludskanov, "Semiotic Transformations (Ts) are the replacements of the signs encoding message by signs of another code, preserving (so far as possible in the face of entropy) invariant information with respect to a given system of reference" (5).

If Catford's theory of translations based on M.A.K. Halliday's "Categories of the Theory of Grammar," Nida's theory draws upon Transformational Generative Grammar (T.G. Grammar) and Componential Semantics. It is further indebted to Case Grammar proposed by Fillmore and Systemic Grammar proposed by M.A.K. Halliday. Both the theories propose to study translation scientifically. In other words, they take translation as a kind of linguistic bridge-building.

Speech Act Theory came into existence with the publication of J.L. Austin's William James lectures for 1955 under the title *How to Do Things with Words* and that gave rise to a Speech Act Theory of Translation. This theory of translation yields a topology based on the nature of the act—that is, the use of the language towards a specific end or its 'pragmatics.' Within this model the translator is taken both as an Addressor and an Addressee, R.D. Doctor illustrates this concept in the following way:

> Within the framework of a Speech Act Theory, at least two or more than two participants are involved which at least one is the Addressor and the other(s) is/are the addressee(s). The Addressor is the source of the message/code and hence also the source of the Illocutionary Act, since behind his utterance one can discern his intentions or his implications. The Addressee is the receiver of the message and hence is exposed to the perlocutionary value of the utterance. Curiously owing to the phenomenon of Communication Feedback the addressor also undergoes the perlocutionary effect: an often exploited comic situation is one in which a liar ends up himself a believing that his lies are truth, falling victim to his perlocutionary powers. The situation of the Translator is somewhat akin since the Translator is simultaneously Addressor and Addressee as Fig. below reveals:

| Addressor 1A | | Addressee 1 | | Addressor 1B | | Addressee 2 |
|---|---|---|---|---|---|---|
| Author/Text (Source-Text) | → | Translator as Reader | ↔ | Translator as Translator | → | Reader of Target-Text |

> The Translator is an Addressee insofar as the Source-Text is concerned and an Addressor from the point of view of the Target-Text and its Reader/Addressee. But the resemblance between the Translator and the Addressor victim of his own perlocutionary skill but rather that of another addressor, the author. It cannot be denied that the Translator does have a Perlocutionary feedback but that is relatively less important than the Perlocutionary impact of the Author/Text Addressee. It would hence be more correct within the framework of a Speech-Act Theory to visualise the Translator as a Clearing-House for all three kinds of Speech-Acts. This concept is not new: Mounin (1963) called the Translator a "filter" through which the Source-Text was passed onto the Target-Text. (Talgeri and Verma 153-54)

Different translation theorists have defined translation variously. Each theory has its validity—however limited it may be. Like the theories of criticism which can never be absolute, no theory of translation can be total and absolute. No translation of literature can be final, for literature itself is elusive. Even then, attempts to divide translation studies bear fruit for they facilitate our understanding of the translation process. James S. Holmes' division of translation studies in the following way is very useful:

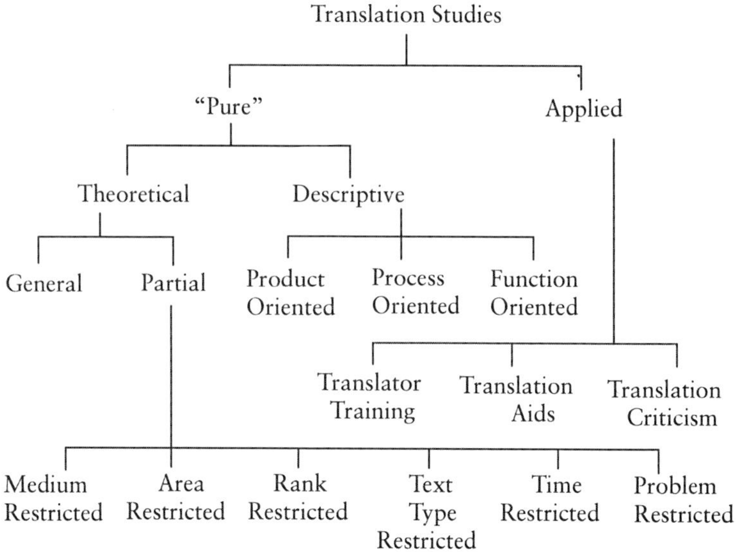

Apart from the theories of translation, the commonsense will tell us that translation is a essentially process of being 'carried over' and its success depends on how far an SL text is adequately 'carried over' to the TL text—semantically, culturally and linguistically. This process of being 'carried over' poses problems for the translator and often baffles him (Toury 21).

Mythlological words like the 'tandav nritya' (tandav dance) of Lord Shiva, 'Kalaharan' (taking away of strength) of Arjun by Lord Krishna, 'Laxman Rekha' (Lines drawn by Laxman), etc. are untranslatable. The translator has to transliterate these words with footnotes to explain their meanings. The English word 'shame' for Indian words (Bengali and Oriya words) 'Lajya' and 'Laja' seems to be inadequate. 'Lajya' is used in a positive sense, whereas 'Laja' (shameless) is used in a derogatory sense. Culture words pose special difficulties for the translators. If a story is based on a cultural act, the difficulty arises right from the translation of the title and ends with a kind of mistranslating the message of the story. I would like to quote U.R. Annathamurthy at some length to illustrate this point:

> Doing *Ghatashradda* into English was my first experience of translation. I had to choose one of my Kannada stories for the B.B.C. third programme, and I assumed I was safe in choosing this story as it had a simple and straight narration which I thought would come through even if the nuances of the language were lost in the process of translation. A Brahmin boy, aged about ten, tells his story here, without being aware of the implications of his story. He is living in a *Pathashala* getting his Vedic lessons after his *Upanyanam*. He is home-sick and is looked after by a young widow, the daughter of his Guru. He does not know that this widow is pregnant, and a school teacher from the town, now living in the *agrahara*, is her secret lover. The other older boys who are also learning the Vedas know this. They are jealous of the innocence of this boy, and of his special relationship with the young widow. There develops a mother-son relationship between the boy and the widow, who is under severe pressure to get an abortion by her unscrupulous lover, and lives in terror of being found out by the elders of the

> *agrahara*. There is an abortion in the end which the boy witnesses. It is thus a story of the crisis of growing-up, the inevitable loss of innocence (of the boy as well as of the woman). The other boys rag the innocent boy, and try to destroy him but the boy survives and the woman loses her caste. The ritual that throws her out of caste is called "Ghatashradda," in which a mud pot is broken, and her last rites are done as if she is dead for the community. The ritual at the end is symbolic, but it is enacted at various levels (the poet/the belly/the pots used in everyday ritual/the Vedic hymns celebrating fertility and the opposite of it practised by the community, etc.).
>
> My first difficulty was with the title. Since I could not find an equivalent for the word, I called the story INITIATION at the instance of my teacher and supervisor in England, Prof. Malcolm Bradbury, a well-known novelist and critic. The title INITIATION made it a story of the boy rather than of the community; he became the focus. My original title has the boy, the woman and the community in continuous and unbroken focus. My hope that the story would come through because of its simple narration was belied because my friend and I who jointly translated the story found ourselves adding explanatory phrases, thus introducing an unnatural element into the boy's consciousness. We gave the story to a Canadian friend, who tried to shorten and tighten it and the whole thing ended up in a garbled version. (69-70)

It would not be out of place to record here that of all the arts, literature alone is beset with the problems of translation because it uses languages as its medium of expression. In music, dance, painting, architecture and sculpture there is no room for translation for none of these use language as its medium of expression. Moreover, a literary work more often than not carries a subtext with the surface text. And that creates a major problem in literary translation. The nature of language has a great role to play in the process of translation. For example, Sanskrit and Latin are highly inflected languages but English is not. In English, word-order is of paramount interest. So to translate from Sanskrit or Latin into English or *vice versa* creates problems for the translators.

While concluding the book two important things come to mind—that is, what is the status of translation and how to rate a translation (*i.e.*, what is his position?). Paradoxically enough, we always translate our thoughts and ideas into a language. In fact, we don't think in a vacuum—we think in a language. Since language is not the fully adequate medium to translate our thoughts and ideas—we do not express ourselves completely in a language. No writer or person has been able to say what he wanted to say because of the elusive nature of language. That means something is also missed in the original creative writing. Hence, there is no point in saying that since something is lost in translation, translation should not be undertaken. If one looks at translation from this angle, Brendan Kennedy's assertion of translation as 'the art of fascinating failure' and George Steiner's contention that 'translation is both possible and impossible—a dialectical antinomy characteristic of esoteric argument' (89) seem to be a little misconceived. Translation is always possible and even one of the greatest books of the world, *The Authorised Version of the Bible* is a work of translation. When translation fails to 'carry over,' transliteration and transcreation help us to tide over the problem. The next question is where to place a work of translation—in the source language or in the target language. Maybe, in both and neither. Sometimes it suffers the fate of mythical Shakuntala being disowned by both the parents. A work of translation if taken as a version of SL text, belongs to SL. Otherwise, it may be taken as an addition to TL and hence, forms a part of TL. But the best thing is to take translation as 'literature three' having an independent status of its own. Being modelled on original creative writing, 'translation' does not cease of the creative. Translation is both creative and intuitive and therefore, can be taken as 'literature three' written in TL and based on SL.

What are the qualifications of a translator. Long ago speaking of the qualifications of a critic, Eliot said that he must be in possession of facts. In other words, without learning and scholarship, no one can become a critic, though anybody could be a creative writer (if he has the spark of creativity within him) without any formal learning or training. A translator must have inwardness with both the language and the culture of SL and its people. He should also possess an insight into the use of SL and TL. Unless one is thorough with the language and culture of a particular country, he cannot be successful as a translator. If a critic is now considered as not merely an interpreter but a co-creator, the translator is not a mere renderer of an SL text into a TL text, but a co-creator. He creates something new, while translating an SL text. Hence, translation has become creative. My closing remarks will be that translation is possible and it is 'literature three,' if you will. And the translator should have inwardness with both the languages—SL and TL, to make his job easy. He should combine in him the skills of a polyglot and a linguist. Translation is what translation does, isn't it?

Finally, what does translation do? It transmigrates the SL Text to the TL Text. Hence, we can call translation as transmigration and rightly so. That is why, it is bound to be different from the original if not in substance, at least in form, because it is the re-birth of the original. And what is the purpose of translation? It is basically meant for the readers who can't read the original. If a reader who knows both the languages of the SL Text and TL Text, he is in a position to make a comparative study of the original and the translated text. Thus, Comparative Literature issues out of translation. Good and bad translations are matter of opinion. Translator could be creative and imitative but not exactly like the creative original writer. That is because, the translator has a text before him but the creative writer has none—he creates the text. That does not mean the role of the translator could be minimized. If creative writer is the mother, the translator is the foster mother. The text needs both to exist in two languages. Translation is both the medium and the message. It saves the ancient texts from extinction and gives a new lease of life to the original text.

## WORKS CITED

Ananthmurthy, U.R. "On Translations," *Cygnus* 2: 2 (1981). Print.

Bassnett-McGuire, Susan. *Translation Studies*, London and New York: Routledge, 1991. Print.

Holmes, James S. "The Name and Nature of Translation Studies," *Translation Across Cultures* ed. Gideon Tour. New Delhi: Bahri Publications Pvt. Ltd., 1987. Print.

Kennelly, Brendan. "On Translating from Gaelic," *The World of Translation*. New York: PEN American Centre, 1987. Print.

Ludskanov, A. "A Semiotic Approach to the Theory of Translation," *Language Sciences* 35 (April 1975). Print.

Nida, Eugene. "Science of Translation," *Language* 45 (1969) 483-98. Print.

Raiomond D. Doctor. "Towards a Speech Act Theory of Translation," *Literature in Translation* Ed. Pramod Talgeri and S.B. Verma. Bombay: Popular Prakashan, 1988. Print.

Steiner, George. *After Babel: Aspects of Language and Translation*. London: OUP, 1975. Print.

# Bibliography


**Journals (special numbers on translation)**

(i) *Critical Practice* 1:2 (June 1994).

(ii) *Cygnus* 2:2 (1981).

(iii) *Indian Literature* 37:4 (July-August 1994).

(iv) *International Journal of Translation* (New Delhi: Bahri Publications).

(v) *Journal of Contemporary Thought* (Summer 2002).

(vi) *Journal of Literary Studies* 13:1 (June 1989).

(vii) *Perspectives: Studies in Translatology* (1993) 1.

(viii) *The Literary Criterion* 22:2 (1987).

**Books**

Adams, R.M. *Proteus, His Lies, His Truth.* New York: W.W. Norton, 1973. Print.

Apter, Ronnie. *Digging for the Treasure: Translation After Pound.* New York: Peter Lang, 1984. Print.

Arnold, Matthew. *Essays by Matthew Arnold.* London: Oxford University Press, 1914. Print.

Arrowsmith, W. and Shattuck, R., Eds. *The Craft and Context of Translation.* Austin: University of Texas Press, 1961. Print.

Bassnett, Susan. *Camparative Literature: A Critical Introduction.* Oxford: Blackwell Publishers Ltd., 1998, Print.

Bassnett-McGuire, Susan. *Translation Studies.* London: Routledge, 1991. Print.

Bassnett-McGuire, Susan and Lefevere, Andre, Eds. *Translation History and Culture.* London: Pinter, 1990. Print.

Bassnett, Susan and Harish Trivedi, Eds. *Post-colonial Translation: Theory and Practice.* New York: Routledge, 1999. Print.

Beaugrande, Robert de. *Factors in a Theory of Poetic Translation.* Amsterdam and Assen: Van Corçum, 1978. Print.

Belloc, Hilaire. *On Translation.* Oxford: The Clarendon Press, 1931. Print.

Bigunet John and Schulte, Rainer, Eds. *The Craft of Translation.* Chicago: University of Chicago Press, 1989. Print.

Brault, J. and Blodgett, E.D. *Transfiguration.* Toronto: Buschek Books, 1998. Print.

Brislin, W.R., Ed. *Translation—Applications and Research.* New York: Gardner Press Inc., 1987. Print.

Brower, Reuben, Ed. *On Translation.* New York: Oxford University Press, 1966. Print.

Catford, J.C. *A Linguistic Theory of Translation.* London: Oxford University Press, 1974. Print.

Cohen, J.M. *English Translators and Translations.* London: Longmans, Green & Co., 1962. Print.

Congrat-Butler, Stefan. *Translation and Translators: An International Directory and Guide.* New York: R.R. Bowker Company, 1979. Print.

Davis, K. *Deconstruction and Translation.* Manchester: St. Jerome Publishing, 2001. Print.

Davie, Donald. *Poetry in Translation.* Milton Keynes: The Open University Press, 1975. Print.

Day Lewis, C. *On Translating Poetry.* Abingdon-on-Thames: Abbey Press, 1970. Print.

Devy, G.N. *In Another Tongue: Essays on Indian Literature in English.* Madras: MacMillan, 1993. Print.

Duff, Alan. *The Third Language.* Oxford: Pergamon Press, 1981. Print.

——. *Translation.* Walton Street: Oxford University Press, 1989. Print.

Eco, U. *Experiences in Translation*. Toronto: University of Toronto Press, 2001. Print.

Finlay, I. *Translating*. English Universities, Press, 1971. Print.

Forster, Leonard. *Aspects of Translation*. London, 1958. Print.

France, Peter, ed. *The Oxford Guide to Literature in English Translation*. Oxford: Oxford University Press, 2000. Print.

Frawley, William. *Translation: Literary, Linguistic and Philosophical Perspectives*. London: Associated University Press, Inc., 1984. Print.

Fulter, F. *The Translator's Handbook*. The Pennsylvania State University Press, 1984. Print.

Gentzler, Edwin. *Contemporary Translation Theories*. London: Routledge, 1993. Print.

Graham, Joseph F., ed. *Difference in Translation*. Ithaca: Cornell University Press, 1985. Print.

Guenthner, F. and Guenthner-Reutter, M., eds. *Meaning and Translation, Philosophical and Linguistic Approaches*. London: Duckworth, 1978. Print.

Holmes, J. *The Name and Nature of Translation Studies*. Amsterdam: University of Amsterdam, 1975. Print.

——. ed. *The Nature of Translation: Essays on the Theory and Practice of Literary Translation*. The Hague: Mouton, 1970. Print.

Holmes, J., Lambert, J. and Lefevere, A., eds. *Literature and Translation*. Louvain: ACCO, 1978. Print.

House, Juliave. *A Model for Translation Quality Assessment*. Tubingen: TBL Verlag Gunter Narr, 1977. Print.

Jacobson, Eric. *Translation, A Traditional Craft*. Copenhagen: Nordisk Forlag, 1958. Print.

Jussawalla, Adil. *New Writing in India*. Harmondsworth: Penguin Books, 1974. Print.

Karunakaram, K. and Jayakumar, M., eds. *Translation as Synthesis: A Search for a New Gestalt*. New Delhi: Bahri Publications Private Limited, 1988. Print.

Kelly, L.G. *The True Interpreter: A History of Translation Theory and Practice in the West*. Oxford: Blackwell, 1979. Print.

Lefevere, Andre. *Translating Poetry, Seven Strategies and a Blue Print*. Amsterdam: Van Gorcum, 1975. Print.

——, ed. *Translating Literature: The German Tradition from Luther to Rosenzweig*. Amsterdam and Assen: Van Gorcum, 1977. Print.

Merwin, W.S. *Selected Translations* 1968-1978. New York: Athereum.

Mattiesson, F.O. *Translation—An Elizabethan Art*. Harvard University Press, 1931. Print.

Mukherjee, Sujit. *Translation as Discovery and Other Essays*. New Delhi: Allied Publishers Private Limited, 1981. Print.

——. *Translation as Recovery*. Ed. Meenakshi Mukherjee. Delhi: Pencraft International, 2009. Print.

Nida, E. *Towards a Science of Translating*. Leiden: E.J. Brill, 1964. Print.

——. *Language Structure and Translation*. Stanford: Stanford University Press, 1975. Print.

Nida, E. and Taber, Charles. *The Theory and Practice of Translation*. Leiden: E.J. Brill, 1969. Print.

Niranjana Tejaswini. *Siting Translation*. Hyderabad: Orient Longman, 1995. Print.

Newmark, P. *Approaches to Translation*. Oxford: Pergamon Press, 1981. Print.

——. *A Text Book of Translation*. London: Prentice-Hall, 1988. Print.

Popovic, Anton. *Dictionary for the Analysis of Literary Translation*. Department of Comparative Literature, University of Alberta, 1976. Print.

Postgate, J.P. *Translation and Translations*. London, 1922. Print.

Rafel, Vicente, L. *Contracting Colonialism: Translation and Christian Conversion in Tagalog Society under Early Spanish Rule*. Ithaca: Cornell University Press, 1988. Print.

Raffel, Burton. *The Art of Translating Poetry*. Pittsburg: Pennsylvania State University Press, 1988. Print.

Ramakrishna, Shantha, ed. *Translation and Multilingualism: Post-colonial Contexts*. Delhi : Pencraft International, 1997. Print.

Ray, Mohit K., ed. *Studies in Translation*. New Delhi: Atlantic Publishers, 2002. Print.

Richards, I.A., ed. *On Translation*. Cambridge: Harvard University Press, 1959. Print.

Robinson, Doug. *Western Translation Theory: From Herodotus to Nietzsche*. Manchester: St-Jerome Publishing, 1997. Print.

Robinson, Douglas. *The Translator's Turn*. Baltimore: Johns Hopkins University Press, 1991. Print.

Rossetti, D.G. *Poems and Translations*. London: Oxford University Press, 1968. Print.

Savory, Theodore. *The Art of Translations*. London: Cape, 1957. Print.

Schaffner, C., ed. *Translation in the Global Village*. Celveton: Multilingual Matters, 2000. Print.

Schulte, Rainer and John Biguenet. eds. *Theories of Translation: An Anthology of Essays from Dryden to Derrida*. Chicago: Chicago University Press, 1992. Print.

Selver, Paul. *The Art of Translating Poetry*. London: Job Baker, 1966. Print.

Singh, A.K., ed. *Translation: Its Theory and Practice*. New Delhi: Creative Books, 1996. Print.

Simon, Sherry and Paul St. Pierre. eds. *Changing the Terms: Translating in the Post-colonial Era*. Ottawa: University of Ottawa Press, 2000. Print.

Smith, A.H., ed. *Aspects of Translation*. London: Secker and Warburg, 1958. Print.

Snell-Hornby, Mary. *Translation Studies: An Integrated Approach*. Amsterdam: John Benjamin, 1988. Print.

Steiner, George. *After Babel: Aspects of Language and Translation*. London: Oxford University Press, 1975. Print.

Steiner, T.R. *English Translation Theory*. Amsterdam and Assen: Van Gorcum, 1975. Print.

Talgeri, Pramod and Verma, S.B. eds. *Literature in Translation*. Bombay: Popular Prakashan, 1988. Print.

Toury, G., ed. *Translation Across Cultures*. New Delhi: Bahri Publications, 1987. Print.

——. *In Search of A Theory of Translation*. Tel Aviv: The Porter Institute for Poetics and Semiotics, 1980. Print.

Toury, Gideon. *Descriptive Translation Studies and Beyond*. Amsterdam and Philadelphia: John Benjamins, 1995. Print.

Venuti, Lawrence. *The Translator's Invisibility: A History of Translation*. New York: Routledge, 1995. Print.

——. *The Scandals of Translation: Towards an Ethics of Difference*. New York: Routledge, 1998. Print.

——. *The Translation Studies Reader*. New York: Routledge, 2000. Print.

Warren, R., ed. *The Art of Translation Voices from the Field*. Boston: North Eastern University Press, 1989. Print.

Weissbort, Daniel, ed. *Translating Poetry: The Double Labyrinth*. Iowa City: University of Iowa Press, 1989. Print.

Will, Frederic. *The Knife in the Stone*. The Hague: Mouton, 1973. Print.

Wilss, W. *The Science of Translation: Problems and Methods*. Tubingen: Gunter Narr, 1982. Print.

——. *Translation Theory and Its Implementation*. Tubingen: Gunter Narr, 1984. Print.

# Index